Reason for the Season

Ministerial Reflections
On Personal Grief, Suffering and Loss

Reason for the Season

Ministerial Reflections
On Personal Grief, Suffering and Loss

Edited by
Bob R. Agee
and
Roger D. Duke

 Founders Press

Committed to historic Baptist principles
Cape Coral, Florida

Published by

Founders Press

Committed to historic Baptist principles

P.O. Box 150931 • Cape Coral, FL 33915
Phone (239) 772–1400 • Fax: (239) 772–1140
Electronic Mail: founders@founders.org or
Website: http://www.founders.org

©2010 Founders Press

Printed in the United States of America

ISBN: 978–0–9785711–8–4

Cover design by Ryan Harrison.

Contents

Contributors iii

Preface v

Acknowledgements ix

Dedication xi

"I Asked the Lord that I Might Grow" xiii

Part I: Ministers' Contributions 1

1. God's Enabling Grace in the Path of Suffering 3
    Roger D. Duke

2. Cancer and Pastoral Care 13
    L. Rush Bush

3. How to Deal with a Life-Threatening Illness 25
    Bob R. Agee

4. Exalting Jesus in the Life and Death of a Loved One . . . 33
    Curtis McClain

5. A Journey in Providence 45
    David Miller

6. Listening to the Silence 55
    Danny Blair

7. Serving God through the Storm 65
    Fred Luter

8. God's Sufficiency and Abundant Grace 72
    Michael Spradlin

9. Hope that Helps When Life Hurts 80
    Paul Barkley

Part II: Physicians' Contributions 91

10. Facing the Realities of Suffering and Death 93
    Scott Morris

11. A Country Doctor's Perspective on Grief and Suffering . . 100
    Wayne Rhear

Contributors

Part I: Minister's Contributions

Chapter 1

Roger D. Duke is Assistant Professor of Religion and Communication at the Baptist College of Health Sciences, Memphis, Tennessee. He writes from the perspective of how his 26 year old "special needs" son has formed his perspective and ministry.

Chapter 2

L. Rush Bush was the Dean of the Faculty at Southeastern Baptist Theological Seminary, Wake Forrest, North Carolina. Bush wrote about what it meant to him personally when he, as a minister, was battling the effects of cancer, radiation treatment, chemotherapy and physical therapy. He lost the battle with what he called the "terrorist" of cancer.

Chapter 3

Bob Agee is President Emeritus of Oklahoma Baptist University and the Retired Executive Director of the International Association of Baptist Colleges and Universities. Agee reflects on what his survival of four bouts with hairy cell leukemia has meant to him and others to whom he has ministered personally.

Chapter 4

Curtis McClain is the Chair of Religion and Bible at the Missouri Baptist University, St. Louis, Missouri. He writes from the perspective of how his father's murder by a homeless person several years ago has shaped him for ministry.

Chapter 5

David Miller is an Ordained Baptist Minister in Siloam Springs, Arkansas, who maintains an active evangelistic and at-large preaching ministry across the southeast United States. He reflects on how his only son's recent auto accident and recovery has shown him anew how providence can be "bitter-sweet."

Chapter 6

Danny Blair is the Director of the Disabilities and Theology Programs at California Baptist University. He writes from the perspective of what it means to marry someone who was born deaf and how this has affected his spiritual formation and view of the ministry.

Chapter 7

Fred Luter is the Pastor of the Franklin Avenue Baptist Church in New Orleans, Louisiana. Luter reflects on his pastoral and personal roles during Hurricane Katrina and the post-Katrina aftermath and how he dealt with his Franklin Avenue Baptist Church parishioners.

Chapter 8

Michael Spradlin is President of Mid-America Baptist Theological Seminary in Memphis, Tennessee. His reflection comes out of his experience as a young father who nearly lost his wife from complications from childbirth soon after the birth of their second child.

Chapter 9

Paul Barkley is Associate Professor of Religion and Psychology at the Baptist College of Health Sciences in Memphis, Tennessee. Barkley reflects as a parent who has dealt with a daughter with lifelong Cystic Fibrosis who has recently received a double lung transplant.

Part II: Physicians' Contributions

Chapter 10

Scott Morris, MD, MDiv is Founder of the Church Health Center in Memphis, Tennessee. He is a physician as well as an ordained minister. Morris established this center for the "under insured" and indigent patients who seek or require primary health care in the Memphis downtown area. He offers unique insights as a physician and a minister on the ongoing suffering of the poor.

Chapter 11

Wayne Rhear, MD is a physician with a private practice in Alamo and Jackson, Tennessee. He has focused on the needs of geriatric patients in the "nursing home" context for nearly thirty years. He writes from a Christian physician's perspective on grief and suffering of those who are geriatric patients in the nursing home and hospice environments.

Preface

When this work was first conceived, it was thought that Christians who are not ordained to full-time ministry might appreciate some insights into the little realized fact that ministers suffer in the same way as everyone else. Many times a minister will convene, console, and comfort at some calamity, bereavement, or other appointment ordained by the Hand of God. But who consoles and comforts the minister as he goes through his own "dark night of the soul?" Who acts as pastor to the pastor? It was during the incubation of this thought that one of the co-editors[1] came across some spiritual formation readings of Dr. M. Robert Mulholland, Jr.[2] He was smitten by Mulholland's "Definition of Spiritual Formation."[3]

---

[1] Roger D. Duke.

[2] The Asbury Seminary web page, http://www.asburyseminary.edu/faculty/bob-mulholland/ says concerning Mulholland: "Dr. Mulholland is a nationally known biblical scholar, listed in *Who's Who* in the Methodist Church, *Who's Who* in Biblical Studies and Archaeology and *Who's Who* in Religion. He is the author of several books on Scripture and spiritual formation, including his latest book, *The Deeper Journey: The Spirituality of Discovering your True Self* (InterVarsity Press, 2006). He is currently a consulting editor for *The Journal of Spiritual Formation and Soul Care*, an elder in the Kentucky Conference of the United Methodist Church and a member of the Wesleyan Theological Society and Society of Biblical Literature, Dr. Mulholland is a frequent speaker at Bible and spiritual renewal conferences, and serves as a faculty member of the Academy for Spiritual Formation." Electronic source cited 12 July 2009.

[3] M. Robert Mulholland, Jr., *Invitation to a Journey: A Road Map for Spiritual Formation* (Downers Grove, IL., Inter Varsity Press, 1993), 15–17.

Because this has become the "heart and soul" of these essays, this definition is stated at length:

> [I]… may [need]… to develop a working definition of spiritual forma-
> tion that has integrity with the scriptural witness to life in relationship
> with God, and let you work out its relationship to whatever other defini-
> tion of spiritual formation you may have adopted.
> …[W]e will develop a fourfold definition of spiritual formation as[:]
>
> (1) a process
> (2) of being conformed
> (3) to the image of Christ
> (4) for the sake of others.[4]

When these special testimonials were recruited, each was selected because it was unique to the Christian ministry. As the selection process came
about for chapter contributors, mostly based on personal or professional
relationships, it became more apparent that there were a greater number
of ministers who had suffered, grieved, lost loved ones, or had an ongoing
condition than had been initially understood. The contributors were asked
to take one part of Mulholland's definition, or the whole, and use it as a
lens through which to reflect and write. Each, in his own way and from his
own perspective, adds a dynamic to the discussion of spiritual formation
that, we hope, will comfort all who suffer and read these reflections. We
especially hope that these personal "testimonies" will speak to the hearts of
the gospel ministers during their "valleys" and "shadows of death."

In one of his many works on Christian piety, Michael A.G. Haykin
quoted a somewhat lengthy personal letter of the Anglican Divine John
Newton. It had been Newton's custom to mentor young ministers and aid
them in their pastoral ministry and proper biblical understandings. One
such minister was John Collett Ryland. Haykin recalls one such instance:
"During his early years of ministry Ryland received much solid and judi-
cious advice and encouragement from John Newton."[5] Haykin continues:
"One gets a good understanding of the way that Newton … helped …
when Ryland's … first wife Betsy was on the verge of death."[6] Newton's
letter to Ryland during these dark days may best capture the heart and soul
of what the editors and contributors seek to do with this humble volume:

---

[4] Ibid, 15.

[5] Michael A.G. Haykin, "A Cloud of Witnesses: Calvinistic Baptists in the
18th Century" *Evangelical Times Perspective* No. 3 (Faverdale North, Darlington,
England: Evangelical Times, 2006), 45–51.

[6] Ibid, 48.

My dear friend, I feel, but I do not fear for you. The God whom thou servest can support and deliver you. He is all sufficient, and his promise sure. Plenty of advice is at hand, but I dare not offer you much in this way. You are in the heat of a trial; I am at present quiet. It would be easy for me to press patience and resignation upon you, and to remind you that a pardoned sinner ought never to complain. You could speak the same language to me, if I were in your case, and you were at ease. Yet though we may and ought to compassionate one another under our various trials, and to speak with tenderness where the heart is wounded, there are truths which, if trouble hides them from our view, it is the office of a friend to recall them. You and I are ministers. As such, how often have we commended the gospel as the τὸ ἕν ["the one thing" that is needed], affording those who truly receive it, a balm for every wound, a cordial for every care!

How often have we told our hearers, that our all-sufficient and faithful Lord can and will make good every want and loss! How often have we spoken of the lights of his countenance as a full compensation for every suffering, and of the trials of the present life as not worthy to be compared with the exceeding abundant and eternal weight of glory to which they are leading! We must not therefore wonder, if we are sometimes called to exemplify the power of what we have said, and to show our people that we have not set before them unfelt truths which we have learnt from books and men only. You are now in the post of honour, and many eyes are upon you. May the Lord enable you to glorify *him*, and to encourage *them*, by your exemplary submission to his will!

You are doubtless allowed to pour out your heart before him, and even to pray for Mrs. Rylands's recovery, and I will join with you as far as I dare.... I pray for her, that he may enable her quietly and cheerfully to commit herself into his hands; and I pray for you, that you may do the same. You may be assured he will not try you beyond what he enables you to bear. If it be for your good, especially for your chief good, his *glory*, she shall recove; he will restore her, though a hundred physicians had given her up. If otherwise, I doubt not but he will help you to say, Thy will be done. And hereafter you shall see that his will was best. ... Accept this hasty line as a token of my sympathy. I was not willing to wait till I could find more leisure. May the Lord bless you both. And may we all so weep as becomes those who expect, ere long, to have all our tears wiped away.

I am sincerely and affectionately yours,

John Newton[7]

Within these essays the reader will encounter varied circumstances: a minister with uncertain life expectances due to cancer, a minister who

---

[7] Ibid, 48–49.

"flat-lined" from a heart attack and lived, a minister who lived through and continued to minister in the aftermath of Hurricane Katrina, a minister who has ongoing and severe chronic health issues with his children for thirty years, a minister who has lived with a "special needs" child for more than a quarter-century, a minister who has been confined to a wheelchair for many years and continues to preach, a minister whose father was murdered, a minister who married a woman who was deaf, and yes, even a minister who died of cancer. The Christian is bound to suffer in this life—but our suffering is always in light of the cross. Nothing can separate us from the love of God who did not spare His own Son. His power is sufficient to help in times of suffering. In the midst of the most difficult times, He makes His presence known and through His love, He provides strength and hope in the midst of the storm.

We the contributors and editors of this simple volume, pray that the "God of all peace" will use this as an instrument to bring a measure of His grace, peace and rest to you as you hopefully encounter God's presence here.

Soli Deo Gloria!
Bob R. Agee
Roger D. Duke
Summer 2009

Acknowledgements

As the editors worked with the people and their stories as told in the pages of this book, we were touched deeply by their depth of faith and their ability to take the difficult events of life and allow God to use them to help them grow and develop spiritually. Our empathy stemmed from the fact that the two of us are indeed "fellow sufferers" whose courage and faith have been tested in the fires of life-threatening illness and the heavy weight of caring for a loved one through challenging circumstances.

It is not always easy to reflect on and talk about parts of the journey which have led the contributors to this work through pain and struggle. Early on Bob tried to turn his encounter with cancer into a story or sermon that he shared on several occasions only to find each time was emotionally draining. The compensation for the emotional struggle in delivering the sermon came in the fact that he never told the story without people responding by telling him that they or a member of their family had just been diagnosed with cancer or had been battling cancer for some time. Invariably more than one person would thank him for talking about the journey. He came to realize that on those rare occasions when he felt led to share the message, God was leading because He knew someone would be there who needed what was said.

Our lives have been enriched as we read the individual stories and sensed the heartbeat of those willing to reflect on and write about their journey. Each contributor, out of his own unique perspective, was so open and transparent. Physical and emotional struggles are very real for everyone, and the minister of the gospel is not exempt. We have learned that faith does not protect us from bad things. It does, on the other hand, equip

and empower us to deal with life's valleys with a special kind of courage and hope. On more than one occasion we have stood at the hospital
bedside or at the graveside with families who had been smacked in the
face with a hard fist of suffering. We have watched the way people handle
their difficulties and are absolutely convinced that a personal relationship
with Jesus Christ and the ensuing constant presence of a loving Heavenly
Father make a phenomenal difference in the way people process their experiences.

Those of us who shared our stories in this volume would be quick to
tell you—ministers suffer and struggle too. Just like those great souls in
the pews, we walk through the "valley of the shadow of death" and reach
out to the promise that He is with us every step of the way. We don't offer
"quick fixes" or shallow platitudes about just having to accept things without thought and the search for a sense of God's presence.

To each colleague who contributed to *Reason for the Season*, the editors
offer our genuine heartfelt gratitude. Our prayer is that people's faith will
be strengthened and each reader will find a source of affirmation and comfort that will help them deal with what life throws at them with renewed
courage and strength.

We would also like to thank Dr. David Dockery, President of Union
University, for suggesting the title, *Reason for the Season*. He made this sug-
gestion while on the Union University's "Retrace the Reformation" tour to
Europe with Dr. and Mrs. Roger D. Duke in the Summer of 2007.

Bob R. Agee, PhD
President Emeritus
Oklahoma Baptist University

Roger Duke, DMin
Professor of Religion & Communication
Baptist College of Health Sciences

THIS VOLUME IS LOVINGLY DEDICATED TO THE MEMORY OF

L. RUSS BUSH

PREACHER, SCHOLAR, THEOLOGIAN, PHILOSOPHER,
FRIEND, DEVOTED HUSBAND AND FATHER,
AND FAITHFUL FOLLOWER OF JESUS CHRIST

L. RUSS BUSH
1944–2008

Revelation 2:10 "... Be thou faithful unto death ..."

All Christians suffer. The New Testament tells us to expect it. We may experience the suffering of persecution, the suffering of temptation, the suffering of loss, the suffering of sickness, and a suffering that we are virtually sure will lead to death. But God, who raises the dead, makes us more than conquerors, even in the moment that we are accounted as sheep for the slaughter, through Him who loved us by giving Himself for us. This volume in that broad sense is dedicated, therefore, to all Christians.

In a specific sense, however, it is dedicated to one of the contributors whose suffering in a particularly aggressive type of cancer led to his death shortly after his work for this volume was completed. L. Russ Bush left this earthly life in January 2008. He was a Christian theologian, philosopher, preacher, defender of the faith, seminary administrator, and encouraging friend. As one may easily discern from the content of his article, Russ always operated under the assumption that Christian truth bore immediate relevance to Christian suffering. He worked to demonstrate that in his classes in philosophy and apologetics, and he lived that in his fight with, to use his graphic image, the "terrorist" that finally took his life. All the way through his crisis he had hope, expressed optimism in conversations, and used every means at his disposal to beat back the enemy death in order to gain a bit more time to serve Christ and complete projects that he believed would help further the cause of Christian truth. When the doctors finally told him that nothing more could be done than had been done and that his time was short, his family said, "Let us pray for you." He responded, "No, let me pray for you." And he asked for God's gracious providential care over all of those that depended in greater or lesser degrees on his presence. In a talk with his wife, Cindy, he requested that at the funeral she be confident and assured and that she look good. She did both. With the hope that this volume may help many readers face the crisis of suffering with the grace and courage that he did, we dedicate this volume to him.

Tom J. Nettles, PhD
Professor of Historical Theology
The Southern Baptist Theological Seminary

I Asked the Lord that I Might Grow

I asked the Lord that I might grow
In faith, and love, and every grace;
Might more of His salvation know,
And seek, more earnestly, His face.

'Twas He who taught me thus to pray,
And He, I trust, has answered prayer!
But it has been in such a way,
As almost drove me to despair.

I hoped that in some favored hour,
At once He'd answer my request;
And by His love's constraining pow'r,
Subdue my sins, and give me rest.

Instead of this, He made me feel
The hidden evils of my heart;
And let the angry pow'rs of hell
Assault my soul in every part.

Yea more, with His own hand He seemed
Intent to aggravate my woe;
Crossed all the fair designs I schemed,
Blasted my gourds, and laid me low.

Lord, why is this, I trembling cried,
Wilt thou pursue thy worm to death?
"'Tis in this way, the Lord replied,
I answer prayer for grace and faith.

These inward trials I employ,
From self, and pride, to set thee free;
And break thy schemes of earthly joy,
That thou may'st find thy all in Me."

Hymn composed by John Newton, #36 in Book III of *Olney Hymns* (London: W. Oliver, 1779), taken from electronic source http://www.hymntime.com/tch/htm/i/a/iaskedtl.htm, 16 July 2009. See also *The Works of John Newton*, vol. 3 (Edinburgh: The Banner of Truth Trust, 1985), 607–608.

Part One

Ministers'
Contributions

I

God's Enabling Grace In the Path of Suffering

Roger D. Duke

When this volume of essays was first conceived, it was like most of God's work done in the lives and hearts of Christ's followers. It had a beginning and a continuation process, but the outcomes are generally unknown to us and only known to our Sovereign Lord. In the midst of any catastrophic issue comes many life questions that the theologians and philosophers from time immemorial have been unable to answer adequately. The main one of these is the "Why?" When these times of catastrophe come—as they surely will—it is natural and normal to begin a long and deep introspection process. This reflection is sure to become more acute especially for one who would become a "fully devoted follower of Jesus Christ."[1]

In times of introspection we all parse out the "why" question into many of its component parts. We want to assign blame! We want to find a reason! We want to know the cause for the predicament where we presently find ourselves! More times than not, we must come to grip with the fact that whether we want to admit it, some of the issues may lie within us. In this quagmire of doubt and self-examination, we long to find who we are—really are. Howard Thurman, in his *For the Inward Journey*, gave

---

[1] Sam Shaw, "Our Goal is to Lead All Peoples to Become Fully Devoted Followers of Christ," Germantown Baptist Church, Germantown, TN, 1998-2006. This was one of Germantown Baptist Church's core values adopted under Shaw's tenure of pastoral leadership.

some helpful insight that could encourage the questioner. He stated: "The desire to be one's self is ever present. Equally persistent is the tendency to locate the responsibility for the failure to be one's true self in events, persons, and conditions—all of which are outside and beyond one's self."[2] This self-examination, or search "to be one's self," will be a major consideration of this short essay.

This reflection will be governed by three dynamics. First, I will reflect on our son's condition and how it has impacted my ministerial and wider life. Secondly, Howard Thurman's volume, *For the Inward Journey: The Writings of Howard Thurman*, will be employed because of its devotional and lasting personal impact. Thirdly, Robert Mulholland's "Definition of Spiritual Formation"[3] will serve as a reflective lens through which these thoughts have passed as this work was composed.

Personal Ministry Formation

I was really young when I was "called" into the ministry. I was not so much young in age as I was in maturity and idealism. I had no idea what I would be facing when we left Nashville, Tennessee, on January 1, 1982 to come to Memphis to attend Mid-America Baptist Theological Seminary. And I certainly had no understanding how it would impact my wife, who was six months pregnant at the time, and our two year old daughter. I had been trained as a union pipefitter, steamfitter, and welder. This thing of seminary was altogether new to me. Could I do the rigorous work that Mid-America demanded? That remained to be seen.

In the midst of the stresses and strains of balancing family and seminary life—typing academic papers, taking tests, tackling the lack of money, preaching on the weekends, working seemingly never-ending menial jobs to provide for the family—there was the surprise of a second seminary baby. Roger (Dale) Duke, Jr. was born on June 30, 1983. Although he was a "Jr.," he was called by our common middle name in order to preserve his own identity.

My wife and I were completely immersed in this new-to-us thing called "the ministry." As I moved through Mid-America's Diploma of Theology (later renamed Associate of Divinity) program, God began to move in my

[2] Howard Thurman, *For the Inward Journey: The Writings of Howard Thurman* (Richmond, ID: Friends United Press, 2002), 85.

[3] Robert Mulholland, *Invitation to a Journey* (Downers Grove, IL: InterVarsity Press, 1993), 15–17. Mulholland defined Spiritual Formation: "Spiritual formation is the process of being conformed to the image of Christ by the gracious working of God's Spirit, for the transformation of the world."

heart that I should go on and further my education. So the tedium previously described above seemed to go on endlessly. I would go as a candidate to churches seeking to call a pastor, and there would be nothing to come of the preached "trial sermon" or pastoral interview. I worked part-time jobs but eventually found a full-time job in order for us to live and pay the bills. I even found a small country church where I could preach and minister on the weekends. All the while I held to the conviction that real academic education was a goal and end for the ultimate God would have me do.

During the hustle and bustle of these first days of ministry and education, my dear wife was a real "soldier of the cross." She never once complained about our financial or ministerial circumstances or the long-haul educational road that lay ahead for us both. Because I had no prior academic preparation, it would take at least ten to fifteen years to complete my master's and doctoral work. It was during these early days that we began to have problems with Dale's health. Linda has a wonderful mind and great powers of observation. She is trained as a scientist and worked for years in medical research at Vanderbilt University. She began to sense, as well as see, that something was fundamentally wrong with our third child. I might add that this was the son that every man wants so desperately to have. At about the age of six months he was not sitting up as he should and also not doing other things that his two sisters had done at the same age.

This is when Linda and I began the arduous task of having him examined, evaluated and shuttled from doctor to doctor. This seems, in retrospect, that it was a never-ending process. What made it so much more acute were the facts concerning his myriad of diagnoses. In the physical and psychological evaluations, it was discovered that he had a small brain. This bears the technical medical name of *microcephaly*. He was also developmentally delayed, as Linda had surmised. He was hypotonic in muscle tone and development. They also told us that he was mentally retarded. In the midst of these "medical guesses" as I have learned to refer to them, one of the teams of doctors and psychologists told us the worst possible news—news that I can hardly repeat even now because the depth of pain! Still! We were told that he had a degenerative brain disorder that would eventually take his young life.

In the twenty five years following, Dale has had around 15 surgeries for various and sundry issues—so many episodes and surgeries that it is hard to remember them through the haze of age. In retrospect, I truly wish that I had kept a journal or diary. No doubt, those remembrances would have been precious now. He had so many hospital stays and nearly died on numerous occasions. We are blessed at the time of this writing that we have not had a life-threatening "event" for some four years. But there will always be another chapter to be written concerning his life and care.

As you can imagine, this news devastated us. The severity of the totality of these circumstances would henceforth form us ministerially, vo-
cationally, emotionally and familiarly. I began learning one major thing
during those long and dark days at the first of Dale's health issues. I share
this with the "Spiritual Aspects of Care" classes I regularly teach at Baptist College of Health Sciences. In this class we investigate the dynamics
and connections between the body and spiritual components of persons
in times of grief and suffering. I argue that the body cannot be affected
without the inner person—the spiritual person—also having repercussions
at some level. What I share is very simple indeed and yet so very profound:
There is an inseparable symbiosis between the inner person and the outer
person. We truly are physical as well as spiritual beings that together make
up the whole. Then I warn my students. Never tell your patients that you
know or understand how they feel. You do not! You cannot possibly know
how they feel at a given point in time. But through all of those feelings
of *denial, anger, bargaining* and *depression* there finally came some level of
acceptance.[4] It did for us.

Robert Mulholland: A Definition of Spiritual Formation

One of the main problems I had in the beginning of my call and preparation for ministry was the lack of understanding God's way of doing
things long-term. It seems He was not concerned with time and issues
surrounding that context as much as we are. I found it very disconcerting
when the health issues we faced with Dale confronted us again and again.
When all this began I was young and ready to go! Give me something
to do and I would do it in straight order! Even in my perpetual degree-
seeking process, I only needed to know where the next school was, what
the next degree was, who the next professor was, what the next assignment
was, what were the next books I had to buy, and how to finance it all. I was
in "attack mode" throughout those years.

But God is in the process mode and not the punctilliar mode. He
knows that we, as humans, take much time to change. He also knows that
that change comes slowly and incrementally for us. We are much more like
the Queen Elisabeth II luxury liner which takes much time and lumbers
along, rather than a ski boat that darts and turns about quickly. More than
likely, we spent a great deal of time getting here—like the QE II, and it is
going to take a great deal of time for us to get out of our present predica-

---

[4] For a fuller discussion of the "Kubler-Ross's Stages of Grief" Theory see:
Myers, D. *Psychology*, Fourth Edition (New York: Worth Publishing), 143.

ment. It is the process of the time taken that forms our character. Character is formed in a very, very slow process. For some of us, more than others, it takes a lifetime. There are those followers of Christ who are "quick studies." But I am not one of those. I am confident that I would not, nor could not, have learned what little that I have learned without the grace of God working through this long and drawn-out process of Dale's health issues.

Part of Mulholland's definition, that of *being conformed to the image of Christ*, is found right in the middle of one of the most wonderfully perplexing passages of Scripture in all of the New Testament. Here the Apostle Paul wrote: "And we know that all things work together for good, to them that love God, to them who are the called according to His purpose" (KJV). This is the midst of the context of Paul's "Five Golden Links of Salvation"—foreknowledge, predestination, calling, justification and glorification. It is not our concern here to deal with this issue theologically. However, the idea of being conformed to the image of Christ seems to be set in the midst of what God is doing from eternity past into eternity future; i.e., the changing of the believer into the character of His dear Son— our Lord Christ. Suffering is bound to come. And it comes for different reasons. We all suffer. The Scriptures also declare in Job 5:7: "Yet man is born unto trouble, as the sparks fly upward" (KJV).

The reasons for humanity's suffering vary greatly. We suffer because of our personal sin and rebellion. We suffer because of the sin and rebellion of others. We suffer because of foolishness and lack of wisdom. We suffer from the results of bad choices. Someone might have a history of a certain disease in his family. They know they should take better care of their health as far as what they eat, exercise, or other personal lifestyle habits. But for whatever reason, they do not follow a good course of health for themselves. Wars come. Young men go off to fight and come home in metal caskets. We get old. Sicknesses unto death come, and suffering attends the sicknesses. Sometimes is it not a "sickness unto death." Sometimes it is a debilitating disease with all of its complications and sufferings. And sometimes a child is born with some measure of disability. In some extreme cases someone may even have to suffer persecution or martyrdom for the Master.

Suffering comes in many forms in this life, even to Christians. But Christians have the opportunity and privilege of magnifying the gospel in the midst of suffering. Our message to the world is that Christ is more valuable than health or comfort or ease. We are willing to face whatever it takes in this life for the joy of knowing and glorifying Him. John Piper declares concerning the Christian's suffering:

> If we would see God honored in the lives of our people as the supreme value, highest treasure, and deepest satisfaction of their lives, then we

must strive with all our might to show the meaning of suffering, and help
them see the wisdom and power and goodness of God behind it *ordain-
ing*; above it *governing*; beneath it *sustaining*; and before it *preparing*. This
is the hardest work in the world—to change the minds and hearts of
fallen human beings, and make God so precious to them that they count
it all joy when trials come, and exult in their afflictions, and rejoice in the
plundering of the property, and say in the end, "To die is gain."[5]

I was once blessed to hear a sermon by Rev. Don Moore, former Ex-
ecutive-Secretary for The Arkansas (Southern Baptist) State Convention.
In this sermon, Dr. Moore stated an alternative definition of grace that I
had not encountered before. He said that grace was, "God's merciful enabling."[6] That concept was very interesting to me. Moore went on to state
the case that by the same grace that we had been converted, it was the selfsame grace that we were to be empowered to live the Christian life.[7] God
had not left us alone unto our own devices. But, how is it that this grace
comes to the believer? What does this grace look like? How will I know I
have this merciful enabling by God for the job or circumstance at hand?

Once again, we can look at Mulholland's definition for guidance. He
states that what God does is done by "the gracious working of God's Spirit." As I have grown (although somewhat slowly and awkwardly at times),
I have learned that God is not necessarily concerned with what is going
on outside of me. He is more concerned with what is going on within me.
I am not saying that God is not sovereign and in complete control of all
of life's circumstances. What I am saying is that for the person to whom
some external issue has caused them some great difficulty, or sickness, or
trauma, or even death, God knows and cares. But there is a "greater weight
of glory" that Paul talks about. That greater weight has to do with the
character formation of His children. That is where "the gracious working
of God's Spirit" comes to bear on the follower of Christ.

One of the great questions the philosophers and theologians have
asked since time immemorial is "WHY?" All of the world religions, all
major philosophical "schools of thought," all Christian theological systems,

---

[5] John Piper, "Preaching to Suffering People," *Feed My Sheep: A Passionate
Plea for Preaching* (Morgan, PA: Soli Deo Gloria Publications, 2002), 242-243.

[6] Don Moore, quote taken from a sermon given at the annual Greater Life
Evangelism conference (G.L.E.A). The G.L.E.A. conference was the homecom-
ing Bible conference held by Evangelist Sam T. Cathey and hosted by the Grand
Avenue Baptist Church, Fort Smith, AR, for Cathey's Board of Advisors and
supporters. This quote is remembered vividly by the author and has had a great
influence in his personal life in the years hence. The quote was *circa* 1981.

[7] See Ephesians 2:8–10.

and every single human being of every hue who ever lived has pondered evil, suffering and grief. It does not seem to have an answer. But the Christian knows that if we cling to our relationship with Christ that we can be changed internally through whatever external circumstance we might be called to suffer for the Savior. The Apostle Paul, the great apostle to the Gentiles declared: "Therefore, we do not lose heart. Though outwardly we are wasting away, yet inwardly we are being renewed day by day" (NIV).[8] The mature Christian also knows that God has a work to do in the world.

Probably more times than not, external circumstances—evil, suffering, grief, or loss—are used of the Father to work in us a conformation to the image and character of His dear son, Christ Jesus. We are then changed, as it were, from the outside in. Then we can be used as tools for His greater purposes as change agents for the *transformation of the world*.[9] It would appear that many (I dare not say most), never get over or get out of the blame they cast upon God their Heavenly Father. They are left bereft of a sense of His love and power and grace in their lives. How hardly do we see someone who recovers and goes on to be involved in this transformation of the world that Mulholland has captured in this succinct definition. The old black preacher declared in his sermon on Job: "God gives (or allows) these things to come to us to make us *better—not bitter!*" [this writer's emphasis] There is something in the world God wants done, and He wants us to be instruments of His transformation power.

Wise and Sure Words

As I have wrestled over the years for some knowledge and consolation in my own spiritual formation journey, I have read extensively in spirituality and devotional readings of many in church history—Calvin, Luther, Teresa of Avila, St. John of the Cross, John Bunyan, Chrysostom, Oswald Chambers, St. Thomas, Charles Spurgeon, et al. All of these have all been "friends" as I have sought answers. One of the most moving devotionals in my own experience has no doubt been John Chrysostom and his commentary on Zechariah 13:9. There the Scriptures declare: "And I… will refine them as silver is refined, and will try them as gold is tried: they shall call on my name, and I will hear them; I will say, it is my people; and they shall say, The Lord is my God" (KJV).

---

[8] See Paul's entire confession in 2 Corinthians 4:16–18.
[9] See citation 3 above, Mulholland's definition of Spiritual Formation.

Chrysostom observed concerning the text:

Refiners throw pieces of gold into the furnace to be tested and purified by the fire. In the same way, God allows human souls to be tested by troubles until they can become pure, transparent, and have profited greatly from the process. Therefore, this is the greatest advantage we have. So then, we shouldn't be disturbed or discouraged when trials happen to us. For if refiners know how long to leave a piece of gold in the furnace, and when to draw it out, if they don't allow it to remain in the fire until it is burnt up and destroyed, how much better does God understand this process! When He sees that we have become more pure, He frees us from our trials so that we won't be crushed and defeated by them. Therefore, we shouldn't retreat or lose heart when unexpected things happen to us. Instead, we should submit to the One who knows best and will test our hearts by fire as He likes. He does this for a reason and for the good of those who are tried. [10]

Through all of this there is one thing that I am learning to be absolutely sure and true. This is the same life lesson that Job learned throughout his trials and tribulations: "Lesson #1—God is God! Lesson #2—I am not!"[11]

Concluding Reflections

Turning once again to Howard Thurman's *For the Inward Journey*, I find words that soothe an old tired soul and allow me to have a sense of peace in my own personal journey. Thurman wrote:

Thomas a Kempis reminds us that in the nature of life, and man's experience in it, that there be what he calls "war and affliction." This is not a note of pessimism or futility—it is rather recognition that conflict [grief and suffering][12] is a part of the life process. Again and again in the struggle a man may experience failure, but he must know for himself even though such is his experience, the final word has not been spoken…. Mr. Valliant-for-Truth in [Bunyan's] Pilgrim's Progress says, "My sword I give to him that shall succeed me in my pilgrimage, and my courage

---

[10] Christopher D. Hudson, J. Alan Sharrer, and Lindsay Vanker, eds., "Tested by Fire" by John Chrysostom, in *Day by Day with the Early Church Fathers: Selected Readings for Daily Reflection* (Peabody, MA: Hendrickson Publishers, 1999), 13.

[11] This is a little axiom that I employ when I have students in the Religion 302, *Spiritual Aspects of Care* class, at the Baptist College of Health Sciences, read the Old Testament Book of Job.

[12] Essayist's Interpolation.

and skill to him that can get it. My marks and my scars I carry with me, to be a witness for me that I have fought His battle who will be my rewarder."[13]

Grief, suffering, war, loss and conflict are all the plight of humans it seems. But how do we deal with them? How do we respond? How should the "fully devoted follower of Christ" react? Should we not respond in a supernatural way? Or even on another plane altogether? We do suffer! That is true. But Paul declares in his first epistle to the Thessalonians that they were to respond in hope: "But I would not have you to be ignorant brethren... that ye sorrow not, even as others which have no hope" (KJV).[14] This hope is not only that which looks forward to the resurrection. It is that hope that empowers us and teaches us of Christ's way in the "here and the now!" It is actually one of the many internal dynamics that the Holy Spirit employs for use as a means for conforming us to the Father's beloved Son—Christ Jesus.

Many, many years ago at a Bible conference, even before I knew the Lord was moving in my heart to follow Him in the ministry, I heard a song. It was a song that gripped my heart and has become my "journey prayer" of sorts. I was foolish enough to pray the song as a prayer and have on some level ever since. I share this prayer now as an indicator of what I think it means to follow Christ on our journey fully, devotedly, and completely—not that I have attained! The song is "Whatever it Takes" by Lanny Wolfe:

> There's a voice calling me
> From an old rugged tree
> And He whispers, "Draw closer to Me
> Leave this world far behind
> There are new heights to climb
> And a new place in me You will find."
>
> For whatever it takes to draw closer to You,
> Lord, that's what I'll be willing to do.
> For whatever it takes to be more like You
> That's what I'll be willing to do.

---

[13] Thurman, *For the Inward Journey*, 59.

[14] See 1 Thessalonians 4:13. It is clear from the passage that Paul is here discussing the "hope of the resurrection." But there is no doubt that this selfsame hope expressed by the believers concerning Christ's resurrection and their own bodily resurrection can be appropriated for the ongoing grinds of this life of grief, suffering, and the spiritual formation these can cause.

Take the dearest things to me,
If that's how it must be
To draw me closer to Thee
Let the disappointments come,
Lonely days without the sun,
If through sorrow more like You I'll become.

> For whatever it takes to draw closer to You,
> Lord, that's what I'll be willing to do.
> For whatever it takes to be more like You
> That's what I'll be willing to do.

Take my houses and lands
Change my dreams, change my plans
For I'm placing my whole life in Your hands
And if you call me today
To a place far away
Lord I'll go and Your will obey.

> For whatever it takes to draw closer to You,
> Lord, that's what I'll be willing to do.
> For whatever it takes to be more like You
> That's what I'll be willing to do.

I'll trade sunshine for rain
Comfort for pain—
That's what I'll be willing to do
For whatever it takes for my will to break
That's what I'll be willing to do
That's what I'll be willing to do![15]

The totality and sum of all these issues for me lies in a statement from Albert Mohler. Mohler said: "There is much we do not understand. As Charles Spurgeon explained, when we cannot trace God's hand, we must simply trust His heart."[16]

---

[15] Lanny Wolfe, "That's What I'll Be Willing To Do," taken from electronic source http://preciouslordtakemyhand.com/publish/christianhymns/whatever-it-takes, 20 February 2009.

[16] R. Albert Mohler, "The Goodness of God and the Reality of Evil," commentary by R. Albert Mohler, Jr., taken from electronic source http://www.albertmohler.com/commentary_print.php?cdate=2005-08-30, 3 February 2009.

2

Cancer and Pastoral Care

L. Russ Bush

Cancer is like a modern terrorist. It hits you out of the blue. It seldom allows you to escape. Sometimes you kill it, and it goes dormant; then, reappears. Even the name is enough to frighten us. The fear of death is very real, even to Christian believers. Will it hurt? How and when will death come? How can I care for those that depend on me? Can I afford the treatments?

I am a seminary professor—a spiritual caregiver for many. A pastor even more serves as a spiritual caregiver. I have been diagnosed as having cancer. How do I continue in this role, or must I resign my classroom or pulpit? As a spiritual leader and as one whose life often functions around hospital and homebound visitation, how will I encourage my people and yet be honest with them? How many details do I reveal to them? How many more diet letters and special advice notes can I read from people who love me? When others get better and I do not (or the other way around), how does that affect my opportunities to witness? How do I respond to the wide variety of cancer types that we face in today's world? God loves His preachers and pastors, so why does He let this happen to them? Why should He allow such a harsh disease to affect any of us? Is it random or purposeful for cancer to spread the way it does?

More questions than we can answer! Thanksgiving 2005, I came home from an accreditation meeting in Charlotte with a droopy face on the left side. Thinking it could have been a mild stroke, we went to the hospital and soon I was diagnosed with an aggressive form of cancer that had already begun to spread (six places in my brain and other places). I was told by the experts that I had two months to live, at the most. We immediately started radiation on the brain, then a round of radiation on the main tumor in my chest. Then I was put immediately on a strong chemotherapy for several weeks. A scan showed a new spot inside my spinal cord, and that was assumed to be the final blow. We tried more radiation of the spine, then more chemo-therapy. The chemo and physical therapy have continued, and I write this two years after my initial diagnosis. I still have the cancer (new spots in the brain), but God has given me more time than was first promised and a new treatment option has been offered, the so-called "gamma-knife." God is so good. But everyone does not get the good reports I have had. I know that, and I am grateful to God for His special blessing on me. How much longer, I don't know. I simply trust Him day by day.

The most common initial reaction to learning that your disease is terminal (whether it is cancer or heart disease or any of several others) is fear and perhaps anger or despair. Biblical counselors must not overlook this reality. It is an almost uncontrollable reaction that many have, even those who previously had strong faith.

Words alone do not solve the problem, but it is obvious that the most common greeting from a heavenly being in the Bible is "Fear not" or "Be not afraid." Jesus spoke against worry: "Your Father knows that you have these needs."

Christians are told to bear one another's burdens. The burden of a terminal disease goes beyond the disease itself, but the very language is frightening to many people. For many it is the first time they have ever faced the reality of death (certainly their own death).

These people need assurance that God is very much there for them. As a Christian community, we do not see death as the end. Christ says He has prepared a place for us, and He promised that He will someday return to take us to this place. (His personal return for us is the answer to the apostles' question, "How will we know the way"?) So death is not the end for the Christian believer. Christ will come for us when our time comes.

Nevertheless, we know that many suffer unto death, and we know we do not want to experience pain or otherwise struggle in death. The pastoral counselor must know what is going on behind the outward appearance of the counselee. "I'm doing fine" they always say, and some are. They adjust. They strongly trust God's power to sustain and heal. And they often have strong family support. Thank God for all of that, but the reality of death eventually settles in on them as it does on all of us.

A wife, not often being the family provider, has many concerns about her future, and the husband always worries whether he has accumulated enough wealth to care for her after he is gone. This is a huge issue for him even when she has been handling some of the financial matters all along. Does she know how to pay the bills? Does she understand the obligations the family has? Is there a trustworthy person who can help her as she picks up this burden? Some women handle money better than the men do, but not all. What is her age? Is she employable? Does she have loyal children to assist her? And all of these questions are there for the husband if the wife dies first. Where is your will? Has it been updated recently? No man ever thinks he has enough, and this makes for a high level of stress in both husband and wife (and, to be honest, in children who have lower incomes usually and may feel as if family medical bills, even with insurance, will wipe them out for several years).

Over and again in the Gospels, Jesus is confronted by crowds seeking healing. Some became impatient and tore up a roof in order to lower their friend on his cot to the feet of Jesus in a crowded room. There was never a sickness or an affliction or an evil (unclean) spirit that Jesus could not handle, but there were often things beyond the abilities of His disciples.

Go First to the Gospel

Today we have a vast resource of commentaries on the biblical narratives and many competent essays offering explanations of doctrinal teachings. These passages should be read over time to all terminal patients (and others as well), but the text will simply roll out of the minds of the lost as easily as ice melts on a summer day in the South. Every counselor must first be sure the counselee has heard with clarity (yet without harsh condemnation) the gospel—that all have sinned; that Christ came and died for our sin; and that the wages of sin is death, but the gift of God is everlasting life. If we believe in our heart that Jesus died, was buried, and rose again the third day, and if we affirm with our voice that "Jesus is Lord," then we shall be saved.

Even a pastor should be reminded of these truths, though he has told this story many times to many people. First, since the days of Adam, humans have been growing in the knowledge of good and evil, but we are forbidden to eat of the tree of life and live in sin forever. This is the unmistakable teaching of Scripture, and it matches human experience perfectly well. The issue has never been advocacy of intellectual ignorance, but it is the moral knowledge that comes from obedience or disobedience to the commands of God.

Second, since Adam, all humans have sinned, many in ways unlike that of Adam. Each sin of all the various kinds has the same result. No one today is living in Eden, no one has God's Garden on their land, no one feasts from the Tree of Life. Modern science is a wondrous achievement.

Biological research continues to be Satan's target (with its proposal that all life forms simply evolved from an accidental, undesigned collection of inert chemicals that somehow began to live, life from non-life, leading to reason arising from non-reason). Evolution could be and generally is ignored in chemistry, physics and other disciplines, with no harm to the science. But biologists claim atheistic, naturalistic evolution is the essence of biology and the biological sciences.

Evolutionary theories are all statistically impossible, and they require a large number of chemical events and structures that are impossible in any time frame yet proposed for the age of the universe, and yet the biologists cling to Darwin's theory as the one and only way to think about the origin and development of the reality that biologists study. If we could accept the fact that God is the original life form, that life is incredibly intricate and therefore must have been designed, and that life is sustained by supernatural power, then we would find that biological studies would not be harmed or held back in any way, and that our medical knowledge would increase. Health could be what Jesus seems to have sought, that we might be well and that faith would be involved in the healing, and that we would seek wellness through the name of Christ in association with medicines. James told the early church to visit the sick, to lay hands on them (presence and touching are very important), and to anoint them with oil (use the best medicine of the day).

Third, God allowed Adam (and all of us) to sin, but He personally planned for this ahead of time, and He made a way for us to be saved. In the Garden itself, God sacrificed an animal (probably a lamb, but we do not know for sure which animal kind was used; later Scripture does focus on the unblemished lamb as the preferred sacrificial animal kind). This innocent lamb was slain by the hand of God, and salvation was provided for those who trust Christ and follow Him in faith. By God's grace, our sins were forgiven, and eternal life became a reality.

We who believe the gospel (the good news) have been sealed permanently by God's Holy Spirit. Christ was the Lamb of God. His death was the providing act. Our trust in the atoning death of this embodied Passover Lamb is the means by which we receive divine forgiveness and saving grace. It is by divine purpose alone that we are saved. It is by divine purpose alone that all believers eventually will be healed, kept from Hell, and live forever in our special, prepared place in heaven, doing the special tasks that will be assigned for us based on how obedient we are in the few things assigned to us here (Matthew 25:14–30).

Fourth, the end of earthly life is coming for most of us. It will likely be sooner than we desire. A few will see the glorious coming of the Lord in the skies (I want to be in that number, when the saints go marching in).

Whether or not we are enabled to live until that historical day yet to come, we will all see Jesus when He returns on the clouds of glory. What a day of rejoicing that will be. What better news can we share with those with whom we engage? What hope is there in nirvana, where we supposedly eliminate all of our physical, earthly desires, where we turn from rationality and seem to live in contradictory mental states? Or what hope is there in Allah's heaven, where we must eternally submit to a merciful but harsh absolutist who has no messiah to send to us, no gracious forgiveness to offer us? Allah provides only sensualism as a description of heaven.

Even in Christianity we have fallen for the raft of secular images (e.g. angels with feathered wings sitting on clouds playing harps) that have no basis in fact, offer no hope, and require so little from us. Salvation cannot come from nothingness (and I would argue that neither can "human" beings arise from nothingness by evolution). We offer no one any hope if we are trusting the theory Darwin proposed in the days he lost his faith in God.

Continuing the Conversation

As the counselor points to the hope of the gospel in salvation and becomes convinced that the counselee is trusting in Christ, several points would make up the continuing conversation (not necessarily in this order). First, *God knows the whole story*. God knew me before I was born. He did have and does have plans for me, not only generic plans for all of us but specific plans for me. He has been watching over me all of my life.

I distinctly remember as a child (perhaps three or four years old) I went running to my Daddy who was in front of our house standing by our automobile on the street side. He saw me coming and shouted out "Stop!" I was startled, but I stopped. A car whizzed by. I distinctly remember that for the first time, I realized I could have been killed. I have never before told that story to anyone, and I don't know whether Daddy even remembers the incident, but in my mind it may as well have been yesterday. God even then had plans for me. I never forgot that event, and I never got away from the memory of having my life saved that day. Ask the patient if anything like that ever happened to them or to a friend. God knew them even as a child. His mercy endures.

Two, *God loves us with a deep and abiding love*. As the atheists constantly proclaim (and the recent spate of atheistic books by Dawkins and others seem to make the point endlessly), there is no God as far as we can see. God is not a scientifically detectable entity. He is not an object nor a force field nor anything else we can observe. Thus He must not exist, they say. If He is not natural, then He is not real. But God is (as Christian theologians have often argued) a necessary being, not a contingent being, invisible and holy, all wise and full of all power. His love for us is of a different kind than our love for one another or even for God. His love is pure and unselfish; it is not based on our good works. His love is pure grace. We do not earn it.

God is unseen except through His creation. His creation is not unchanging (as God is), but it changes as He intends so that life exists uniquely as a dynamic reality.

God could have invented a way for us to live without eating, but would you not miss your Thanksgiving and Christmas family meal? Would you see a meal-less life to be better? God knows that life is more than food, and He knows that meals are more than food. God created this system of renewing our energy even though it means some will starve for lack of food. Suffering seems inevitable in a real world.

God is a real being, but He is not dependent upon anything. Contingent things are dependent by definition. Our health depends on many physical factors, but it is not possible to be created without being contingent. A necessary being is not created. It needs no beginning, and it has no beginning. It depends upon nothing but exists as a self-sufficient reality.

When we understand this, we understand why everyone dies, believers as well as unbelievers. We cannot be created and thus be contingent and at the same time be immune to sickness and injury and death. Will we still be contingent beings in heaven? Yes, we were created by God, given life by God, given real bodies by God. But the negatives of contingent beings will be cancelled in heaven because we will be in the presence of God, the source of all life and health. The Bible says He will wipe away all tears, so there must be some tears in heaven, at least at the beginning. What we know for sure is that we will always abide in His love.

Three, *Jesus clearly taught that God knows our needs.* He clothes the earth with flowering plants. But flowers fade, and grass withers, but the Word of God remains. When we are told we have a terminal disease, we understand how earthly we are, and how precious is the Word of God. Sick people, above all others, are open to the gospel. Two thieves were on two crosses on either side of Jesus, but only one believed. So we know that terminal illness does not drive everyone to Christ, but it does give us a great opportunity to speak words of comfort.

Visit the sick and offer to read Scripture to them. If they agree, be very careful what passages you choose to read. It is not necessary to read only Psalm 23 and I Corinthians 15. A sick person might just as well like to hear Genesis 6–9 or Exodus 3 or Luke 19–20. We do not need to express our sympathy by reading only passages about heaven and comfort. Don't ignore such passages, but all Scripture is inspired and useful for us. As a cancer patient myself, I know that it is not only the resurrection stories that are meaningful to me.

Practice reading aloud, and try to read in a natural tone. The oral reading style of most preachers is atrocious. It is often stilted, flat, lacking inflection or proper emphasis. Listen to yourself reading on tape. Professionalism is not out of place here. Clear articulation, no slurred words, proper emphasis, even to the point of accents and slight changes in tone when two or more people are recorded as talking. In other words, read the Bible like it is a living book written for an oral culture (which it is).

God provides His Word because He knows we need it. He provides food, clothing, and health care services because He knows we need these things. You are correct! Not everyone has external resources. Not everyone even has a Bible in their language. Apparently, we have failed to fulfill the Great Commission of Matthew 28. But God's knowledge of our needs is real and total. He is the judge of what is His will. Our terminal illness calls new issues to mind, but God has not forgotten us. He is preparing a place for us, and He will one day send Christ back to earth to show us the way to our eternal home.

Four, *God loves our family members*. God loved Isaac and Jacob. He loved Joseph and Joseph's brothers. Families are often highlighted in biblical stories. It was the mother of Moses who was allowed to help raise him. Jesus was concerned about His mother. Paul, although unmarried, also speaks about husbands, wives and children. There is no question of God's concern for our families.

My cancer requires my wife (or my daughter or someone) to be the major caregiver. Fortunately, my wife is generally in good health, and we are still young enough to manage, but if God loves me—the patient—and He does, then surely He uses the caregiver as a means of expressing that love. Family members are usually closer to the situation of suffering, and they also suffer. Fear not, however, the love of God extends beyond even our fondest hopes. Families are always a part of divine plans.

Five, *God wants the best for us*. It is Satan, not God, who works against us. God sought to lead Israel straight into the promised land, but the people refused. Such a serious rejection of God's best becomes a resounding theme in the New Testament message to the Hebrews. Jesus spoke of how, like a mother hen, He often sought to protect His people by gathering them under His "wings," but the people "would not" be gathered (Luke 13:34). As heaven is described, God wipes away our tears, gives us a heavenly home, and promises to give us responsibilities as we have shown evidence here in this life of our ability to put our gifts to work for the sake of the kingdom (Luke 19:16–18). It is not best for us to experience death from physical illness, but far better to die physically than to die spiritually.

The judgment comes not at the end of our physical life, for our life is not over when we die physically. Our influence goes on. Some are soon forgotten, but others have a lasting influence (for good or ill) and the judgment will take into account not only our life but also our continuing influence. Was our life a blessing to others or did we burden them, cause them to curse us, cause them to hate or ignore God; or did our life point them to heaven and to faith? In today's world, there is such religious confusion. What role in that did our life play? Did our lack of faith hinder the faith of others? Did we point people to Christ or to materialism?

God gives us life that we might have the opportunity to serve Him. He allows illness for the same reason. In each case, what happens to us is what God knows will be best for us. We each have our role to play.

One day we will sit around a campfire in heaven and tell our stories. One will tell of a wonderfully blessed life. All needs were met. No serious sickness until the end. Another will share a similar testimony but with some hardships to be recounted. As we go on around the circle, people will tell of deformity since birth, a life of pain and hardship, and life without enough food or money. Then at the end of this circle of testimony, leading from the best to the worst of life's circumstances, the entire group will join in the chorus: "His grace has been sufficient for me!"

Six, *the Bible is a book of doctrine, but it is also a book of comfort.* We all know that the Bible is the record of the teachings of Jesus and Paul and other apostles. The Old Testament gives us the context of the Ten Commandments. The Bible is our source of Christian teachings. We cannot love God and ignore the teachings of the Bible. But if we see only the doctrinal teachings and we do not see the teaching on comfort, we will have missed an important aspect of scripture. God uses the Bible to rebuke us, but He also uses it to comfort us. Let not your heart be troubled. He is the God of all comfort. Do not worry about what you shall wear or what you shall eat. The Father knows you need these things. He knows the number of hairs on your head. He knows when a sparrow falls. God's grace was sufficient even for Paul's thorn in the flesh. We can count on Him. He gives us His grace without measure.

Seven, *God's love is like none other.* No one cares for me like Jesus. But it is not how much love there is but what kind of love it is. When I say that I love my wife or my children, I usually mean I have a certain feeling or emotion that comes to me when I see them or speak to them or think of them. God's love is not like that. He does not work from emotions as we do. God is an invisible spirit, not a physical being such as we are. His love is based on His omnipotence and omniscience. Ours is not. His love is everlasting, as is He. We are not without failings. There are many ways that

His love differs from ours. We cannot understand love that leads to a cross. We do not possess such love within ourselves. His love is like no other.

So what does it mean to speak of God's love? It means He gave Himself for us. He loves us without emotion but with deep and abiding, self-sacrificial, full-knowledge love. It is a truly spiritual love. We love in response to His love. He first loved us. We usually get something in return for our love. God has no such need. He loves unselfishly.

There is no "He loves me; He loves me not" on our divine daisy. God simply is love. Christ's love saves us from everlasting death. Disease is real, but it cannot cancel divine love. God's love is not based on physical beauty, wealth, health, or personality. It is like none other.

Finding God's love is not our work. He seeks us as a shepherd seeks a lost and wandering sheep. He seeks us as a woman might seek a lost coin. He notices even if our best offering is only two small copper coins. He is not happy with our self-righteous, pompous, braggadocios prayers (especially those on our own behalf).

Our counsel to the terminally ill can easily include these seven realities. Remember: (1) God knows the whole story; (2) God loves us with a deep and abiding love; (3) God knows our needs and will provide for us; (4) God loves our family members; (5) God wants the best for us; (6) The Bible is a book of doctrine, but it is also a book of comfort; and (7) God's love is like none other. Blessed be the name of the Lord.

Conclusion

There is no way to do justice to this topic. God's nature is so great. He is so different from us, and yet the Word of God declares that we are made in His image. We are like Him. We have conscious minds, compassion, grammatical speech, logical rational minds, memory, anticipations and self-awareness. We have the ability to know what is happening to us and in some cases why that is happening. We reach out for help, and we know when people are praying for us.

We know God is real despite the lack of explicit scientific evidence. We believe that God spoke to Adam and to Cain and to Noah and to Abraham. We believe He appeared and spoke to Moses and Joshua. We believe this same speaking God called Samuel, made promises to David, and glorified Solomon's temple. He spoke through Daniel and Ezekiel, and He revealed His promises through Isaiah and Jeremiah. He led the people back from Babylon to Jerusalem, stood on the earth Himself, and taught the multitudes. He enabled the establishment of new churches, and promised to return to conquer illness and death once and for all. Jesus suffered and died, intentionally laying down His life for human lives, something we do not see in monkey societies.

Our attitude toward terminal disease, and the attitude of our caregivers and supporters, is not something that is found in the ape world. We are unique beings, not simply evolved beings. As pastors, our pastoral skills never meet a greater challenge than with the terminally ill. It is not helpful to remind people that "we are all terminal." While true, that offers little comfort. A message of God's love is always needed. By God's grace, it can always be given.

A Personal Letter from Dr. Tom Nettles*
to Dr. L Rush Bush

January 17, 2008

Dear Russ,

Cindy called yesterday to let Margaret and me know what the physicians have said about your health. If they are right, you, sooner than the rest of us, will leave this land of the dying to be in the land of the living among the Spirits of just men made perfect. You will enter into an undarkened, undimmed prelude to the Blessed Hope when you will appear with the Lord in glory.

Russ, you have built your life around defending the truthfulness of the book about Jesus, showing people the land where Jesus walked, and multiplying the evidences of Jesus' victory over sin, death, and the grave. Your heavenly Father is now saying, "Come up here and see the place where Jesus is seated, yet uttering infallible words of intercession for the people he has loved and redeemed."

You have seen the empty tomb, you will see the living Lord; You have seen Jerusalem, the home of David's earthly throne, you will see the eternal throne of David's greater Son; You have cherished the written word, you will soon hear the voice like the sound of many waters saying, "Enter thou into the joy of your Lord."

You have taught us, Russ, to see Christ in the Old Testament, to see him in Creation, to enjoy Him in Providence, and to rest in Him in redemption. Soon you will need no medium, no logical trajectory, no closely reasoned deduction, but your knowledge will be immediate, your senses will be filled, and your pleasure will be pure. You are the Lord's and he has given you all spiritual blessings in heavenly places in Christ. You have been brought to relish them in their fullness before the rest of us.

---

*Dr. Tom Nettles is Professor of Historical Theology at The Southern Baptist Theological Seminary in Louisville, KY.

I will not forget the blessings that have come to me by way of your friendship. Your confidence in Scripture, your love of the church, your zeal for theological education centered on the faith once delivered to the saints, your penchant for independent thinking, your labor through opposition to publish works in service of the truth—I will remember these and seek to help others remember them.

Your faithful mate for life, Cindy, will be cherished by all who have known you as you have labored together. Her love and care for you, and her knowledge of your faithful execution of the stewardship given you, have encouraged all that have known of this heroic struggle of the last two years, as well as your life and ministry.

You have fought the fight, you have kept the faith, and by God's providence you have finished the course. Now there is the crown of righteousness.

Love,
Tom

3

How to Deal with a Life-Threatening Illness

Bob R. Agee

There are few emotions quite like what you feel when a doctor walks into your hospital room and tells you that you have an illness for which there is no guaranteed cure and likely will shorten your life. On September 28, 1990, that is exactly what happened to me.

To say the least, it was unexpected. I guess I had known for several months that something was going on inside me that was different from any physical feelings that I had ever known. For months I had noticed that I bruised more easily and when I got a scratch, it didn't heal as fast. For several years I had been running three miles a day four or five days per week, but after a two month lay-off because of scheduling problems, I discovered that I could not run a lap without being totally out of breath. Even after several weeks back on the track, I could not regain strength or stamina. I chalked these problems up to the fact that I was now past fifty years of age and maybe these are the kinds of things that happen to you when you pass fifty.

In August 1990 I made a trip to mainland China to sign a new agreement with Xinjiang University that would stabilize and strengthen Oklahoma Baptist University's relationship with that institution. As we were coming out of China, I got sick in Hong Kong, and for several weeks following could not seem to get back on my feet. I developed a persistent fever and an uncontrollable cough for which the doctor could not find a cause. My doctor put me in the hospital for tests. Following an extensive battery of examinations and evaluations, he decided to send me to Baptist Hospital in Oklahoma City for a bone marrow aspiration. Even then, the pathologists couldn't seem to find what was causing my blood counts to be so low. They just knew that something was wrong.

Finally, the chief pathologist at Baptist Hospital (who happened to have a son at Oklahoma Baptist University where I was president at the time) determined to identify the problem. He recognized some of the symptoms and decided to try a test for a very rare form of leukemia. Sure enough, that test proved positive. They discovered that I had hairy cell leukemia. And it was in an advanced stage.

The oncologist who broke the news to me was not very encouraging. He told me that at least half of the people who contract this disease live less than three years. It is a form of cancer that destroys blood cells at the point of origin in the bone marrow and, as a result, destroys the immune system. A person seldom dies from the leukemia itself, but is so susceptible to other diseases and infections that one of these usually takes the life of the patient. He told me of some experiments being run with only slight improvement in life expectancy. He also recommended a treatment program that involved taking a form of chemotherapy three times per week.

He prescribed regular doses of Interferon for up to one year's worth of treatment. Because they still could not determine the cause of the high fever and the chronic cough, he decided to put me on Indicin, a medicine I learned later should never be given to a leukemia patient. The side effects of the two drugs were devastating. I began to bleed internally and had to receive several blood transfusions. My system did not tolerate the Interferon well at all, and I felt that I was continuing to deteriorate. The prospects of long-term survival did not look good.

For a person who has been healthy, energetic, and active all of his life, the very word "cancer" or "leukemia" was like getting kicked in the pit of the stomach. The idea that my life was likely going to be shortened by a disease for which there was no reliable cure really brought me low.

Almost immediately, several emotions kicked into gear. First was shock and fear. What would happen to the quality of my life? Who would watch after my family? What effect would this bad news have on them? I was not and am not afraid of death—I settled that long ago when I put my faith in Jesus Christ as my Savior and Lord. But dying was another thing. I have never done that before. That's new territory. What was out there in front of me? As I went through the weeks of dramatic weight loss (twenty-seven pounds in thirty days), blood transfusions, loss of energy, a depth of nausea that is indescribable, and several other unpleasant experiences, there were experiences that were very frightening. I cherish independence and the ability to go and do as I please. I am an outdoorsman who loves fishing, boating, the forests, and adventure. Were these going to be things of the past?

Another emotion that surfaced quickly was a deep sense of the presence of God in my life. I am an ordained minister who felt the call to preach when I was seventeen years old. I became a pastor when I was eighteen and had been in the pulpit regularly for thirty-four years. I spent eighteen years as a pastor and then went to Union University (my alma mater) as Dean of Religious Affairs and Professor of Practical Studies in the Religion Department. During my years of teaching at Union University, I served as interim pastor in one church after another for seven years. During the first nine years of my presidency at OBU, I averaged speaking in fifty churches a year.

All of a sudden I was faced with the haunting question: Did I really believe all of those things that I have told people about God over the years? God had been so good to me. He had blessed me with good health, abundant energy and opportunity. My God was by-and-large a God of the good times. Even though I had known death of loved ones and some heartaches, my life had been marked by much more good than bad. Was my God big enough to handle cancer? Was He big enough to carry me through the sickness and possibly the dying? Within a few hours from the time the doctor walked out of the room an overwhelming sense of peace settled on me. God did not tell me that I would get well. He just made it known to me that He would be there, and we would handle whatever this disease would throw at me. From that moment on, I knew that no matter how dark the valleys or how dreadful the ordeal, He would be there to carry me through it.

A third emotion kicked in alongside the first two. Perhaps it is a reflex that comes from somewhere down deep. Something went off inside me that said, "We're going to fight this thing." I do not like to lose at anything. I decided that I might die from leukemia; but if I do, I will die fighting. I determined that I would learn everything I could about the disease, and I would not rest until I had explored every possibility and fought on every battleground I could find. If there were any way to lick this stuff, I was going to find it. I owed it to my wife and to my kids to do battle.

The strange thing was that all three of those emotions became a part of my prayer pilgrimage. When I prayed, I often found myself wandering back and forth among those three sets of feelings, fluctuating from fear to faith to fighting and back again.

I am happy to report today that the Lord has intervened in my life. When the first treatment process was going about as badly as anything could, a bizarre series of events occurred, all of which, I am convinced, were the Lord's intervention in answer to a lot of prayers offered on my behalf. Within about two week's time, three unrelated events pointed me in a new direction for treatment.

One day in mid-November, I received a note of encouragement from my oldest daughter who lives in Jackson, TN. In the note was a newspaper clipping from the *Jackson Sun* telling about a new drug that was being tested which was having a very positive effect on hairy cell leukemia." Within a few days I received a copy of a report from the *New England Journal of Medicine* that told of this new drug being tested in New York that was proving to be very effective in treating my disease. Some of our faculty from the School of Nursing had found the article in their research and sent the article to me. The very next week I got a phone call from a businessman in Muskogee, Oklahoma, in which he told me that he too had hairy cell leukemia. He had gone to M. D. Anderson Cancer Center in Houston, Texas. There he had received an experimental drug called 2-CDA. He told me that he was in remission and feeling great. He gave me his doctor's name and phone number at the cancer center where she could be reached.

Immediately, I called the number. When I told her nurse my situation, she called the doctor, and she left a meeting to come to the phone to talk with me. She was the most encouraging person I had talked with since the diagnosis. She went on to tell me to have my oncologist in Oklahoma City refer me to her. When I talked to him, he had never heard of the experimental drug and was not aware of the latest research. I asked him to refer me to M. D. Anderson, which he did by the next day.

The drug was in an experimental stage and was being tested at three cancer research centers in the U. S. It was administered intravenously for seven straight days, twenty-four hours a day, after which the IV was removed. Then I began the waiting process. The treatment was administered in early December 1990. By February, the evidence suggested that the drug was working, and by May I was declared in complete remission.

It would be nice if I could report that it remained in remission since that time, but my pilgrimage has been marked by three recurrences of the disease. The good news is that progress continues to be made in developing effective treatments for the various forms of adult leukemia, particularly the chronic forms. With each recurrence—1997, 2001, and 2004—the doctors have been able to treat the disease; and it goes back into remission. I often say that I am alive today because of the prayers of God's people, the wonders of medical science, and the miracle working grace of God.

In April 2007, I suffered a near-fatal heart attack in which I went into cardiac arrest four times over a two-hour period. Fortunately, there was a cardiologist on call when the ambulance arrived in the early morning hours, and she was able to open the blocked arteries. When I regained consciousness in ICU on a ventilator, I was surrounded by my loving family, and the room was filled with an overwhelming sense of the presence of God. My first thought was, "Here we go again. I've done battle before and God has never left my side. We'll simply do battle again and I'll trust Him for the outcome, whatever it is."

Through God's abundant blessing, I have had a marvelous quality of life in between occurrences of the leukemia and following the heart attack. Since retiring from the presidency of Oklahoma Baptist University in 1998, I have been able to remain active in teaching at Union University and consulting with colleges, universities, private academies, churches and other non-profit organizations. I live with the haunting reality that the leukemia will return every few years, but the oncologists are so diligent at monitoring the disease. Through regular blood tests and planned visits to M. D. Anderson, we discovered it early and can make preparation for whatever treatment is required. Medical science continues to research and find improved ways to treat both the chronic and the more acute forms of leukemia and lymphomas. For their diligence and dedication I am deeply grateful.

The lessons learned from four bouts with leukemia and a major heart attack are far too numerous to recount in a single chapter or even a single book. As I have dealt with life-threatening illness for more than eighteen years, I have reached some conclusions that could be helpful to others. I will elaborate upon some of them.

The Importance of Family and Friends

It was such a blessing that I did not have to deal with the tough times alone. With each round of chemotherapy, my wife and daughters went through their own period of agony. Their prayers, their encouragement, and their proactive approach to searching for things that would be helpful to me stirred in me new courage to deal with each occurrence as a "player" and not a "victim." Friends beyond number have taken time to call or write each time the news went out that I was dealing with the leukemia again. There is probably no blessing, beyond the blessing of the grace and presence of God, quite like the blessing of family and friends.

Don't Assume That Your Doctors Know All They Need to Know

We tend to assign to doctors the status of omniscience, and that is not fair to you or the doctor. One of the leading oncologists in Oklahoma City did not know about the most current research and the possibilities that were emerging from the successful tests done with the experimental drug. He also did not know that a leukemia patient should not receive medication that caused internal bleeding. Then you realize that you should not assume that doctors know all they need to know. One of the great blessings has been that the doctor to whom I was referred in 1990 at M. D. Anderson continues to be my doctor. She is so diligent and caring that I feel completely confident in her judgment and recommendations. She does not mind my questions and my efforts at interpreting blood tests and is most encouraging.

Be Informed

I suppose it is my nature, but I wanted to know all I could learn about this disease that was new to me. I thought leukemia was leukemia. As I became a student of the illness, I learned that there are several chronic forms of leukemia and several acute forms. I searched every source I could find to learn all I could about hairy cell leukemia." I also realized that some doctors do not tell their patients all they need to know and that the treated cannot absorb all the information the doctor gives in one session. Some doctors may be uncomfortable with a patient asking questions and insisting on knowing possibilities. But it is important for the patient to probe and ask so he or she can deal more effectively with the effects and side effects of the illness as well as treatments. I know a lot more about adult leukemia today than I ever thought about being interested in knowing. Determine to be as knowledgeable as possible about your body and about the disease with which you are dealing.

Prayer Is the Key to Emotional and Physical Stability

Early in my spiritual pilgrimage I became convinced that one of the most important disciplines I could develop was the discipline of daily conversation with God. There were times over the years that I felt an unusual sense of His presence as I dealt with victories, blessings, threats, and occasional bad times. I was so grateful that when I needed Him, I did not have to wait and prayer was not a new thing for me. As the disease increasingly limited my physical ability to go about my normal routine, I rediscovered the joy of becoming a student again of prayer. For example, my awareness of prayer recognized that prayer should be persistent, seriously personal, totally honest and open. When I prayed, there was no time for religious games. I could express my fears, talk about my pain and discomfort, plead for help, intercede for my family and their anxiety, and praise Him for His presence. My experience with a personal God who cares and to whom I matter made each occurrence a time of spiritual renewal.

Determine to Fight

A fighting spirit stands a better chance of surviving a life-threatening disease than does a fatalistic resignation to the worst case scenario. You owe it to yourself and to your family to do battle with the illness. I had never thought about the threat of dying young until the leukemia showed up. Not really knowing how long I might live or what the process of deterioration and dying would be like, I began to ask God for courage and dignity as I faced each phase or each occurrence. I have been around a lot of people in their "dying days," and those who faced dying with courage and grace were such a witness to me. I wanted to be that kind of witness to my family and friends, and still do.

Work to Maintain a Positive, Upbeat Spirit

I am convinced that we can think and talk ourselves into feeling worse and being miserable. I have been around people who did that and I certainly did not want people to remember me for that kind of spirit. As I grappled with the weakness and the deterioration in those first months, I tried hard to emphasize the positive in my conversations. I tried to talk more about hope than about the gloomy possibilities of what was happening. I tried to smile and laugh more than I frowned or groaned. I realized that my negative spirit and my gloomy conversation could actually cause me to feel worse, while a positive spirit and the effort to smile or laugh could help me feel better.

Stay Active

One of my great fears, as the fever lasted so long and the weakness and physical deterioration began to limit what I could do, was the fear of losing the ability to think, learn, or reason. I had read somewhere that high fever over a sustained period could affect the brain cells, and that frightened me. I had invested so much time and effort in getting a good education, the thought that what I had learned might be wiped away was a scary thing. I began to look for things to do. Even though my concentration was affected by the fever and the medication, I made myself read both fiction and professional books. I looked for things I could do with my hands—light manual labor—that would allow me the satisfaction of knowing that I was doing something productive. During the times of weakness and loss of stamina, I have been able to learn a lot about how to use the computer. Being able to research and write during those times have been therapeutic. While it may be questionable to some family members or friends, that I did not suffer damage to brain cells, I think I retained some functionality even in the worst times.

Exercise

Having been active and involved in sports all my life, it bothered me greatly to see the muscles disappear and the skin color to be more pale that I could have imagined. I still remember the day when I glanced in the mirror as I walked by the dresser in our bedroom and noticed how frail I looked and that I was shuffling rather than walking. The shock of that sight gave me a new determination to find ways to exercise and keep up as much strength as possible. I found exercises that I could do, even in bed— like leg lifts, knee bends, use of light dumbbells, and simply flexing arms, legs and hips. A physical therapist recommended the use of the Schwinn Airdyne stationary bicycle as a way to rebuild muscle tone in my legs, arms, shoulders, and back. I really think the effort to regain strength and stamina helped in the recovery process. Whether it did or not, the exercise made me feel stronger and better able to handle the difficult times.

Conclusion

I asked an elderly friend who had faced all sorts of physical problems but maintained a positive, upbeat spirit: "What is your secret?" She replied: "I decided that when the body began to deteriorate, it was time for the spirit to begin to grow." What great insight into the way to deal with life-threatening illness or circumstances! The wonderful truth for a child of God is that God is able and more than sufficient to supply our every need, even through the most trying times. He can use our physical suffering to deepen our spiritual growth and trust in Him. Our greatest need is Christ. Knowing Him is worth more than anything we can possess in this world, even health, stamina, or life itself. We can say with the Apostle Paul, "For me to live is Christ and to die is gain" (Philippians 1:21). Either way, we have Christ!

4

Exalting Jesus in the Life and Death of a Loved One

Curtis McClain, Jr.

L ittle did I know that the sermon in chapel would have such a profound affect upon my personal life. Ironically, I was the one preaching it. The text was Philippians 1:27–29.

> Only let your manner of life be worthy of the gospel of Christ, so that whether I come and see you or am absent, I may hear of you that you are standing firm in one spirit, with one mind striving side by side for the faith of the gospel, and not frightened in anything by your opponents. This is a clear sign to them of their destruction, but of your salvation, and that from God. For it has been granted to you that for the sake of Christ you should not only believe in him but also suffer for his sake (ESV).

Did Paul claim that saving faith was a gift? Sure, he did. Did he further claim that suffering for Christ was also a gift? If I read this right, Paul wants us to think about "suffering for His sake" in the same way we think about saving faith. That is, they are both the kind and loving generosity of our gracious God. That thought from verse 29 continues to nourish and fortify my soul.

Just an Ordinary Sunday

January 11, 2004, was a Sunday that seemed very typical. However, the events that started on that day would test my beliefs before a watching world of students, colleagues, fellow church members, and people from our past and even our city—St. Louis, Missouri. On that morning my family went their separate ways to various churches for the Sunday morning services. Dad and Mom went to Broadway Baptist Church, an inner-city church where Dad was serving as their new pastor since November 2003. My wife Patsy and our two daughters, Beth (19) and Meredith (9), left for the First Baptist Church of St. Peters where we were all members. I traveled to Heartland Baptist Church so that I could participate in an ordination service.

After the deacon's ordination service where I delivered the charge and after the meal which followed, I began my drive home. Very soon I was faced with an option. I could go straight home, as was my norm, or I could drive north and visit Dad and Mom. Sometimes they would spend the afternoon at the church. If I had known that they were there (which I did not know), I would have visited them (which I did not do). Upon arrival at the house, I discovered that Mom and Dad were not there. I concluded that they had stayed at Broadway, but would return home soon.

Because it was still early afternoon, Patsy and I left the girls at home and drove to Wal-Mart. As we finished parking, Patsy commented that it seemed unusual for Dad and Mom to be gone so long. She was right. They usually were back home around 3:00 p.m. She further wondered if something had happened to them. I responded that I would not speculate on unknown trouble; however, I had sensed a foreboding ever since that decision to go home rather than go by the church. As we shopped I confessed to her that I too sensed something wrong. We should have heard something from them by now.

The cell phone rang. It was my daughter, Beth. The St. Peters (Missouri) police had come to the house looking for Mom and Dad. It took me a few minutes to realize that we needed to go straight home, *tout de suite* (as my Mother would say).

The Road Traveled

J. I. Packer, in his landmark book, *Knowing God*,[1] distinguishes between two kinds of people—balcony dwellers and travelers. People who

[1] J. I. Packer, *Knowing God* (Downers Grove, IL: InterVarsity Press, 1973). I gave this book as a Christmas gift to my Dad when he lived in New England. It

sit on balconies see more of the road of life in one view, but they cannot see over the next hill without leaving the balcony. Travelers may not know what is ahead, but they are on the way of discovery. My Dad was a traveler with Christ by the tender mercies of the Holy Spirit. These are my memories of Dad's life up to his final move to St. Louis.

Born September 1, 1925, to Christian Ray and Margaret Eula Mc-Clain, Curtis was the sixth of their seven children. Granddaddy was a fireman for Oklahoma City. He hated church and fought its influence in his home until the Lord aroused love for Jesus in the later years of his life.[2] Grandmother taught the Intermediates (ages 9–12) Sunday School class and took in ironing so that she could pay Granddaddy's tithe. Dad said that Grandmother visited every absentee of her class every week on foot and dragged him with her.

Dad grew up in the Stockyards area of Oklahoma City, OK. He attended Exchange Avenue Baptist Church when the Lord found him. Often he would recount being nine years old with no thoughts of Christ or his sin when the Lord convicted and convinced him of his need. He surrendered to the Lord's call then and again later when, as a teenager, he was called to the gospel ministry.

After graduating from Central High School, Dad attended Hardin-Simmons for one semester before he entered the United States Army. He served in the artillery and was posted in Hawaii near the end of World War II. He was a forward observer—during an invasion he would go ashore in advance of the attack so that he could spot for the artillery. He told us that his unit was halfway to Japan when President Truman approved the use of the atomic bomb. During his time in the military, he recognized the Lord's protection both physically and spiritually.

An honorable discharge gave Dad both the time and means to continue his education. First, he earned a BA at Baylor University and then a BD at Southwestern Baptist Theological Seminary.[3] While at Baylor he met, courted, and married my mother, Dorothy Lee Scarborough.[4] My mother was his constant companion. She also made sure all of us children understood our role in support of God's call on his life. She was and is instrumental in my understanding of faithfulness and commitment.

At Southwestern, my father served his first Pastorate, Harmony Baptist Church, Atoka, Oklahoma. There my sister, Margaret Ruth, was born. After seminary Dad worked as the chaplain for Baptist Hospital in Musko-

---

was a favorite of his ever since. By the following April he had read it twice.

[2] Ironically, two of his five sons were ministers until their deaths.

[3] The Bachelor of Divinity will become the Master of Divinity (MDiv) later.

[4] Dorothy is L. R. Scarborough's granddaughter.

gee, Oklahoma. That is where I was born. From here the family moved to northeast Arkansas. Dad pastored Corning Baptist Church and then Harrisburg Baptist Church where my brother, Bruce Anthony, was born.

In Harrisburg, Dad encountered strange but powerful opposition. Near the end of a six year ministry, he joined with three other pastors to oppose a county-wide referendum concerning liquor. Even though the referendum lost, all four of the pastors lost their pulpits. We moved to Little Rock, Arkansas, where Dad sold men's suits. Dad and our family went through a discouraging time as far as ministry was concerned. However, we grew closer to each other and we looked for the Lord's answer to life. Prior to leaving Harrisburg, I heard from a friend that we were moving. What I did not know was that members of the church were trying to pay Dad to leave. I asked Dad if it was true. When he did not answer, I asked if God is moving us. Dad had always told us that we move from church to church only when God moves us. He replied "no" to my question and their offer. The result—they fired him.

A few months later in December 1965, Dad accepted a call to pastor the Westmont Baptist Church just south of Memphis, Tennessee (the area would later be incorporated into the city of Memphis). This suburban area experienced rapid growth and a great openness to the gospel. Dad went all over the area witnessing and proclaiming the gospel. This time saw its own forms of opposition. Several women charged Dad with misconduct. This charge proved to be imaginary. My mother initially reacted with laughter. However, this problem paled in comparison with the racial problems the community faced. We witnessed "white flight" on a community-wide scale, race riots at the local schools, segregation in the local churches, and the assassination of Dr. Martin Luther King, Jr. Even though this assassination happened in another part of town, it still wreaked havoc in our area.

Throughout that entire time, I witnessed my Dad face each challenge with biblical guidance. He sought the Bible for direction and then followed that direction and did not use the Bible to justify his actions. He even faced down his own prejudice while confronting the church with theirs. Regardless of their vote, he told them, he would present the gospel and spiritual concern to everyone that came to the door of the church. He also planned to knock on any door regardless of the owner of the house. I witnessed this firsthand several times. One particular instance occurred when our new, next-door neighbor came to the door for marital help. He was a large African-American man in search of a pastor. Dad went home with him, lead him and his wife to the Lord, and won eternal friends as well as terrific neighbors.

In 1973 we moved from Memphis to San Benito, Texas, where Dad would pastor First Baptist Church. The racial make-up changed from 75 percent African-American in our corner of Memphis to 85 percent Latin-American as we lived only thirty miles from Mexico. While this church received repeated opportunities and challenges for outreach, no one in the church cared to reach out. The reigning attitude towards missions limited itself to Mary Hill Davis, Annie Armstrong and Lottie Moon (the three mission's offerings for Texas Baptist). This was in spite of the placement of a foreign country within a short drive. As the church began rejecting Dad's ministry with passive resistance, the Lord prepared the next place for Dad to serve Him. In fall 1978 Dad accepted the pastorate of Glacier Valley Baptist Church in Juneau, Alaska.

Most voices in the Alaska association told Dad that his witnessing methods from "down south" (that is, the "Lower Forty-Eight") would not work here. However, he maintained a consistent declaration of the gospel, prayed aggressively for lost souls and witnessed regularly to see stable fruit. It seems that technique was not the issue, but the means of God's grace that He promised to use. When we depend upon God's Spirit to use God's Word, He is faithful to do with it all He has planned. We need to be satisfied with God's harvest.

From Alaska, Mom and Dad moved back to Oklahoma where he eventually became pastor of Foyil Baptist Church. Foyil, Oklahoma is northeast of Claremore (which is northeast of Tulsa) on famous old Route 66. This little church soon found itself involved in a statewide referendum concerning gambling. The gambling industry sought horse racing in Tulsa. Foyil Baptist used their sign on Hwy 66 to advertise against gambling. Oklahoma approved horse racing. The sign declared that it was time for the church to "take off the gloves." The local news media pounced on this declaration. They asked Dad what he meant. He said that they had appealed to the people, now it is time to appeal to God—in other words to pray. The track was built in Tulsa with attendant stables outside Claremore. Between problems with weather and mechanical mishaps, the track shut down after the first season. It lost too much money.

When Dad reached retirement age, he told the church that if they would provide housing and insurance, he would live on his retirement. He informed them that they could use his salary to pay off the church's debt, as long as they continued to support missions by personal participation and monetary offerings. Though the debt was paid off, the church did not follow through on their commitment to missions and evangelism. Dad resigned and moved to New York State where he moved into a retirement home owned by B'nai B'rith. He intended to help small churches that could not afford a full time pastor.

After a year in New York, he began to pastor the Good News Baptist Church in Middletown, Connecticut. He only left because of my mother's health. He would return to Middletown for a brief stint before making their residence in my home in Missouri.

Lessons Learned from a Faithful Pastor and Dad

I was privileged to watch my father in ministry and to participate with him all my life. The lessons learned from him, both great and small, are too numerous to count. Let me dwell on one overriding lesson which would serve as a guide for all others. Because Christ has control over all of our lives, the Bible must be followed because it serves to communicate His wishes. Dad was no more resolute of character (hard-headed) than any other person of Scottish temperament, nor was he less. However, the Bible always changed his mind.

When the Deeper Life Movement swept through the Southern Baptist Convention and was promoted by preachers like Jack Taylor, Peter Lord, Ron Dunn and Manly Beasley, its greatest effect on Dad was a renewed obedience to Scripture. Daily confession of sin, prayer and bulk Bible reading became part and parcel of our daily activity. Out of this came a guide to thought and behavior which prevented the excesses later associated with the movement. Chiefly, a great sense of the weight of sin and abundant joy of forgiveness resulted in an overriding love for Christ in both of my parents.

In retirement my Dad devoted his time to Bible study. This included taking New Testament Greek for two years, one book at a time, and translating as well as diagramming sentences of the Greek New Testament.

One Sunday, at the age of seventy-seven, Dad came home from the morning worship slightly bothered. He disagreed with part of the sermon, in particular the part where the independence of God was applied to His self-sufficiency. He did not take to the notion that God does not need anyone or anything to complete Him. He argued that God needs us for fellowship and praise. He continued that argument with me that afternoon. When I returned home from work the next day, he took up the discussion again. Dad did not want theologizing nor philosophizing, but Scripture. I turned in my Bible to Acts 17 where Paul says to the Athenians on Mars Hill, "The God who made the world and everything in it, being the Lord of Heaven and Earth, does not live in temples made by man, nor is he served by human hands, as though he needed anything, since he himself gives to all mankind life and breath and everything" (Acts 17:24–25, ESV). After reading this Dad commented that he was wrong and Acts is right!

It was just this attitude that brought me to embrace the Doctrines of Grace. Even though we discussed it often, we did not agree on the

Doctrines of Grace. I asked Dad why he never was angry with me for such disagreement. He reminded me that he taught me to follow my understanding of Scripture. He would not interfere with that obedience to conscience. Prior to his death he too embraced the Doctrines of Grace, not because I did, but because his own Bible study required it. It was this boost in doctrine that caused him to believe firmly that his preaching days were not over. When given the opportunity to pastor at a downtown church, he jumped at it with all his being. Within months this church would serve as the setting of his final full measure of witness to the priceless glory of God as seen in the face of Jesus Christ our Lord.

Encountering Sound Doctrine

J. I. Packer, in his *A Quest for Godliness*, both reminds and warns: "If our theology does not quicken the conscience and soften the heart, it actually hardens both; if it does not encourage the commitment of faith, it reinforces the detachment of unbelief; if it fails to promote humility, it inevitably feeds pride."[5] After college and seminary I would finally submit to just such a process (even though there is still so much more submission to do).

As is typical of many Baptists, I was raised as a closet Arminian. I held to a man-centered theology unawares. Even though I took man as born evil, I did believe he had the ability to believe savingly whenever he chose. I did not think about election at all, but did hold the fact of faith as the condition for salvation. Even though Christ died for everybody and the Holy Spirit does His best to convict us, our decision provides the last connection as linkage to God. Once done, we are permanently God's. I had never heard of Pelagius, Arminius or Calvin, nor had I dwelt on Romans, Ephesians or many other Scriptures in any integrated fashion.

However, this view soon faced important questions. In college I was challenged to decide whether I would have a man-centered or God-centered theology. The more I studied the Bible, the more I perceived God at the center of all things and His glory as the major purpose for this world. The result of man's rejection of God and His purpose was spiritual death. This renders every man unable to come to God or even to desire Him. This revealed saving faith as not inherent to humans, so that it must be a gift to those who are saved. How did God decide to whom He would give saving faith? Since man is unable to merit it, this gift must be a part of His unconditional love for some. So then, God must choose whom to save; Christ

[5] J. I. Packer, *A Quest for Godliness* (Wheaton, IL: Crossway Books, 1990), 15.

died for their sins; and the Holy Spirit wins and keeps them. It all is to the praise of the Trinity's graced-produced glory.

At the same time that God's Word was shaping my thinking, it was preparing me for service. My Bible study continued to encounter passages regarding the suffering of Christians for His name sake. That is, suffering that gives witness to the great worth of Christ and the abundant, unconditional love of His Father. Such passages as Matthew 5:9–12 say as much:

> Blessed are the peacemakers, for they shall be called sons of God. Blessed are those who are persecuted for righteousness' sake, for theirs is the kingdom of heaven. Blessed are you when others revile you and persecute you and utter all kinds of evil against you falsely on my account. Rejoice and be glad, for your reward is great in heaven, for so they persecuted the prophets who were before you (ESV).

Another such passage is Philippians 3:8–11:

> Indeed, I count everything as loss because of the surpassing worth of knowing Christ Jesus my Lord. For his sake I have suffered the loss of all things and count them as rubbish, in order that I may gain Christ and be found in him, not having a righteousness of my own that comes from the law, but that which comes through faith in Christ, the righteousness from God that depends on faith—that I may know him and the power of his resurrection, and may share his sufferings, becoming like him in his death, that by any means possible I may attain the resurrection from the dead (ESV).

Even though these passages have so much more to offer, all they accomplished in me initially was acquiescence, grudgingly, to the probability of suffering. It took a missions book by John Piper to adjust my attitude Godward. In his book *Let the Nations be Glad*, John Piper stated that the purpose of missions is to bring the worship of God to a new locale. As worship is the *purpose*, so prayer is the *power*, and suffering is the *price*. God's way of proving His worth and His love is the suffering of His servants.[6]

God does not just tolerate suffering, but He purposes suffering with joy to communicate to the hearts of men and women. Two thoughts grabbed my attention. One, God would have His servants count the cost of suffering for His name's sake, and they would find the price too little to pay (hence, a joy) to serve Him. Just like Jesus Christ, I must come to the "not

---

[6] John Piper, *Let the Nations Be Glad* (Grand Rapids, MI: Baker Books, 1993), 71.

my will, but Yours be done" attitude. This privilege becomes God's gift for me. So we find encouragement in 1 Peter 4:

> Since therefore Christ suffered in the flesh, arm yourselves with the same way of thinking, for whoever has suffered in the flesh has ceased from sin (4:1, ESV).

> Beloved, do not be surprised at the fiery trial when it comes upon you to test you, as though something strange were happening to you (4:12, ESV).

Two, God's victory over the animosity of this world includes suffering with joy. Now, I must tell you that facing suffering with joy takes an amazing work of sanctifying grace. Still, our example is Christ so 1 Peter 2 reminds us:

> For what credit is it if, when you sin and are beaten for it, you endure? But if when you do good and suffer for it you endure, this is a gracious thing in the sight of God. For to this you have been called, because Christ also suffered for you, leaving you an example, so that you might follow in his steps. He committed no sin, neither was deceit found in his mouth. When he was reviled, he did not revile in return; when he suffered, he did not threaten, but continued entrusting himself to him who judges justly (1 Peter 2:20–23, ESV).

I also heard Piper once construct a hypothetical conversation with the Apostle Paul's friends. They advised him not to go to the next town because there he could only find beating, persecution and possible death. Paul replied, "What's different about this town from any other? That is what I find everywhere I go" [this writer's very loose translation].

While we all understand how the death of Christ illustrates the love of God, how His love is communicated through our suffering seems to elude us. Because God has placed His saving love on believers, God's way of demonstrating His love for sinners—a love that reaches men's hearts while simultaneously expressing the overriding worth of Christ and the glory of God—makes great sense to the submitted Christian. Gratefully, the Holy Spirit's presence provides double duty for us. Even while He empowers the believer to endurance with joy, He works on the hearts of unbelievers. Piper observes:

> The basis for this indomitable joy is the supremacy of God's love above life itself. "The steadfast love of the Lord is better than life" (Psalm 63:3). The pleasures in this life are "fleeting" (Hebrews 11:25) and the afflictions are "light and momentary" (2 Corinthians 4:17). But the stead-

fast love of the Lord is for ever [sic]. All his pleasures are superior and there will be no pain. "In your presence there is fullness of joy, in your right hand are pleasures for evermore" (Psalm 16:11).[7]

Within a few short years, my father would experience just this kind of opportunity. He would do the suffering; I would get to testify.

The Rest of the Story

When my wife and I arrived home, we found a St. Peters (MO) police officer waiting for us. The St. Louis Police had contacted the St. Peters Police in their search for Mom and Dad. A passing motorist encountered Dad's car stopped in the middle of the street in front of the church and called the St. Louis Police. After they discovered the car's ownership, they started their search for Mom and Dad.

Shortly after we arrived home, Mom called from the church. Due to a diminishing mental capacity (later to be discovered as Alzheimer's), she had sat with Dad for nearly an hour until she looked up our number and called us. Within ten minutes the St. Peters Police contacted the St. Louis Police, they contacted paramedics, and Dad arrived at St. Louis University Hospital. He would stay there for five weeks. After another three weeks more at an evaluation unit, Dad was moved to a full care facility where, on March 7, 2004, his body would loose its final battle.

As the events of that afternoon unfolded, we learned that Dad had sent Mom upstairs to the office to rest while he took a man down to the kitchen to make him a sandwich and some coffee. They had befriended this man the previous week and suspected that after he left them, he had broken into the church office to steal money. All week, Dad had him on his mind and in his prayers.

That Sunday afternoon he would try to rob Dad. They struggled and he beat my Dad with a coffee jar. He took Dad's keys, went by the office to tell Mom that the pastor was taking him home, and then tried to steal the car. He drove it into the middle of the street, but could not disengage the parking brake so he just left it there. He was soon apprehended and eventually pled guilty to second degree murder. The next few months I would see the dynamic presence of the Holy Spirit in my own life in addition to many opportunities to witness to His goodness.

[7] John Piper, *Let the Nations Be Glad*, 104.

Suffering for Christ with Joy

As these events began to unfold, even that Sunday afternoon in January, my mind kept hearing Philippians 1:29: "For it has been granted to you that for the sake of Christ you should not only believe in him but also suffer for his sake" (ESV). This verse produced two rather wonderful effects. Initially, my thoughts turned to the perpetrator of Dad's suffering. If this was God's gracious gift like saving faith, how can I have any resentment toward the instrument of this gift? Quite honestly, by God's supernatural grace, I never held any animosity toward the man who did this, even though external temptations questioned this lack of anger. In that very first week, while pondering this unnatural temperament, temptation came and was rebuked. Almost immediately, my phone rang. A member of my Sunday School class, Steve Hughes, called to say that he held me in his prayers. Specifically, he prayed that the doctrine which I had used to comfort and strengthen him would now do the same for me. I told him that God has and is answering that prayer. This lack of hatred would grab the attention of local news reporters, the legal system, my students and colleagues. God produced His own praise by His marvelous grace.

This gift of God revealed God's approval of Dad's sacrifice. It served in my mind as a "well done, good and faithful servant." Not as a praise for Dad, but as a witness to a life that exalted Jesus through the battles and joys of living. When called upon to put a phrase on his grave marker, "Exalting Jesus" naturally rose to the mind. Preaching at his funeral came easy because I knew my task was to exalt Jesus.[8]

Witness—the Ultimate Follow-Through

I have observed in studying some of the Psalms that the real difference between the Lament Psalms and the Praise Psalms was temporal. The Lament Psalms came during a crisis, with an appeal for salvation and promises of praise for that salvation. A Praise Psalm offers fulfillment to that promise. It recalled the problem and God's salvation with joyous praise for His Goodness. This became my trust with the promotion of my earthy Father.

In the public arena I was given repeated opportunities to show the grace of the Lord Jesus Christ.[9] The media told my story without editing

---

[8] I preached through the book of Hebrews revealing and applying the superiority of Jesus Christ.

[9] Reporters told me this story had "legs." There was a public interest that exceeded local stories of its type. This is why it was covered so often.

out the gospel. Even at Dad's funeral, a TV camera fed film to the local stations. They showed particular interest in the testimonies of African-American Christians for a Caucasian pastor. Such is God's grace to replace hate with love.

At Missouri Baptist University where I teach, repeated opportunities for witness came. Twice I spoke in chapel. Because of the God-given events in my life, all the students gave me full attention as I shared the goodness of God. Later, my students would tell me that they felt privileged to witness the connection between my teaching and my life bear out under testing. Isn't God so good; He provided the teaching, the test and the passing of the test and allows us to tell about it?

Privately, I watched as God surrounded us with so many Christian friends to comfort and serve that even now I am staggered at the thought and number. The hospitals provided physical care for Dad and protection from outside pressures for us. The law enforcement system and news media gave consistent and uniform kind treatment to our family. Local pastors covered my classes (except for Hebrew) while I managed nerve central in my home. The First Baptist Church of St. Peters rallied to our need time and again in abundant fashion.

In the aftermath, while my wife cares for my aging mother in our home, I will occasionally still have opportunity to share these events to God's praise. As you read these pages, please do not think more highly of us. We remain the same old miserable sinners who war against the flesh. Think more highly and more often about Christ and His glorious, life-changing gospel.

5

A Journey in Providence

David Miller

I am David Miller and I am 61 years old. I was born in Jasper County, Mississippi, and have lived in Heber Springs, Arkansas since 1969. I have been a country preacher of 43 years. I am not a writer; rather, I am an expositor of the Scriptures. I am accustomed to exegeting a text of Holy Scripture. "Shooting from the hip" or telling "my story" makes me very uncomfortable. Nevertheless, at the request of my friend and with the Lord's permission, I shall offer up my personal reflection on suffering.

Memories of Childhood

I was born with my right arm only partially developed. My parents gave me no special attention because of this. They did not pamper, protect or prevent me from doing normal things that country kids do. I played sports, hunted, fished, climbed trees (with one arm), and enjoyed life to the fullest. My parents divorced when I was only five years old. My father had not been around much, so his absence from my life went relatively unnoticed by me. What did impact me profoundly was the suffering that my mother endured after her divorce. I watched and listened as she worried and sobbed.

What would she do? She had neither job, nor education, nor job training. What she did have was character, integrity and a willingness to work hard. I went to the cotton fields and followed her as she dragged a large cotton sack down each row. Once she cut her foot badly on a sardine can.

Instead of "whining" she wrapped the foot tightly with cloth from a feed sack and continued her work. I remember when our neighbor, Mrs. Thames, came over to tell my mom that a local factory that made electric blankets had called, and they wanted her to come to work for them. I can still see the look of euphoria on her face—she had a job! When the factory closed, Mom worked in housekeeping at a hospital, often working two full-time jobs at a time. She went home to heaven at age eighty-three.

I learned early in life that things are not always easy. Life is often difficult and disappointing. Sometimes it seems that Providence will knock you down and kick you in the ribs. Sometimes Providence is hard and bitter, and yet it is the Providence of God nonetheless.

When I was sixteen years old I began to be affected by a rare form of muscular atrophy—the Charcot Marie Tooth type. In a few short weeks I went from being a captain on the varsity football team to hardly being able to get up the steps at school. Muscular atrophy is a progressive disorder which has affected my arm and legs. At first I was not able to run. Previously, I had run with the top 10 percent of the team, but now I was running with the bottom 10 percent. Soon I had difficulty getting up from a sitting position. Then, I began to stumble and fall often. I wore braces and used a cane. Then I needed someone to hold my arm and assist me in walking. Life is just an adjustment! In 1981 I began using a wheel chair. Then I could not stand at all. Each year for forty-five years I have lost my ability to function in a particular area. This has rendered me more and more dependent on others for hygiene, dressing, grooming, etc. Recently, I have lost my ability to feed myself. This has been the most difficult and frustrating adjustment I have had to make.

While I have wrestled with this debilitating disease, I have not been sickly. Just the opposite, I have only spent one night in a hospital in forty-five years. I am almost never sick. I have not had a virus in years. My stamina and energy levels are very high. I take no medicines at all. I have no pain. I am blessed. My life has been full and rewarding.

Three major epochs have occurred which have given stability and anchored my life—my salvation, my call to preach and my family. I grew up in a rural community. There were three Baptist churches within one mile of my home. Every time I looked up someone was coming to take me to church. I went to Sunday school, to Vacation Bible Schools, to revival meetings. I heard the gospel from my earliest days. On August 5, 1962, the Spirit of God quickened me, granted me repentance with godly sorrow and gave me faith in the blood of Christ. I was converted! I had a new life, new understanding and great joy. Immediately I began to read the Bible, witness the gospel to my friends and grow in the grace and knowledge of Christ.

Ministry and Marriage

Soon after my conversion I began to have thoughts and impressions about preaching. Leaders in my church also discerned the gifts and calling of God on my life. I struggled with the fear of not being able to stand to preach. Am I having these thoughts about preaching because I might not be able to do anything else with my life? This would hardly be a proper motive for announcing a call to the ministry. I wrestled with this for two years until in February 1965, the Lord convinced me that he had called me to preach the unsearchable riches of Christ. I came home from UCA on Friday, visited with my pastor on Saturday, and preached on Sunday!

Two weeks later I drove sixty miles to Snowball, Arkansas and preached to six older women. They called me to be their pastor. The treasurer's name was Miss Icie! While God's Providence had arranged for me to preach in many of the great venues of Southern Baptist life, I must confess that I have never preached with a greater sense of calling or dignity than when I would preach at Snowball. It is a gift of grace to be called to preach. The call of God on my life has given me purpose, focus and great joy.

Should a young man with an arm only partially developed and with an incurable and progressive muscle disease even entertain the notion of having a wife and children? Providence arranges things! In 1964, I completed my last semester of high school in the small town of Scotland, Arkansas. Our church invited Rev. A. L. Emberton to come and preach a "trial sermon." I do not remember much about his sermon that morning. But I remember thinking to myself, "I hope we call him." This was because I had been attracted to his seventeen-year-old daughter, Glenda Faye. I thought she was something else! Our church did call Brother Emberton, and the second week they were there I invited Glenda for a date. I have been happily and enthusiastically dating her ever since! We recently celebrated our fortieth wedding anniversary. She has been my wife, best friend, confidant, critic, encourager, supporter, fellow-laborer and mother to my son. She is a gift of God's grace.

I was the Director of Ministries (DOM) for the Little Red River Baptist Association (of Arkansas) for twenty-five years. In addition, I was an itinerant preacher (revivals, Bible conferences, etc.), and Glenda traveled with me. We always intended to have children, but it never seemed the appropriate time. After thirteen years it dawned on us, if we did not get started, we were going to be Abraham and Sarah all over again! We began to pray; soon our son, Josh, was born in 1981. Some of our family teased us that it was another "immaculate conception." What a joy it has been being a father. I never dreamed I would have so many fulfillments in my life.

Raising a Family

Friends kept telling us, "Boy, your lives are going to change now."They were right! We had to learn that when you hold your baby's cheek next to yours, you will never want to put him down. We learned there was no greater form of entertainment than playing with your child and listening to him giggle and laugh uncontrollably. What fun! We learned the joy of singing great hymns of the faith and teaching memory verses. Glenda taught Josh how to do Bible drills. He won district and state Bible drill competitions.

Our lives changed all right—we spent our time either at home, at church, at work, or playing with Josh. No more evenings out or quiet dinners at home. We had to be at the Optimist's Ball Park for T-ball practice! We loved it! We lived three miles from the ball park and just for the fun of it Josh would ride on the back of my wheel chair and we would go to practice via wheel chair. Other kids and dads envied us for having such exciting experiences.

Because I was always at T-ball practice, the coach decided to let me hand out the bubble gum. Before too long I had moved into the dugout as bookkeeper. A couple of years later I was asked to be an "official" assistant coach. I finished my career as "head coach" with a couple of league championships and many memories. Twelve years later Josh and I still love to talk about those good times. I suppose one memory that stands out more than the league titles was when I arrived late from a preaching appointment and the game was well underway. Even though Josh was 6 feet, 3 inches tall and fourteen years old, when he saw me approaching he ran over and opened the gate to the third base dugout. As I rolled through, he leaned over and hugged my neck with both arms and kissed me on the cheek right there in front of the fans, players and the Lord!

While I had physical limitations, Josh and I always figured out ways to do fun things together. We made trails in the woods that went further than wheelchair batteries will last! Often, Josh had to return home for help because I was out of power, stuck in the mud, or perhaps turned over . . . what fun! We figured out a way to mount a seat on a "four-wheeler" and how to get me strapped in. Josh would drive and I would ride. The fact that Josh was only eight years old at the time prompted Granny Miller to ask if my "cheese had slidden off my cracker?" I invented ways for me to deer hunt. I engineered a stand that would lift me twelve feet high, hold my gun in front of my shoulder, and turn right and left with the flip of a switch. From the time Josh was six years old we hunted together. Deer hunting has been our passion ever since.

Two days after Josh turned fourteen, he got his driver's permit and we took our first solo trip to the deer camp in the motor home. We made many of those trips. We talked about everything: sports, deer hunting, girls, sex, the Bible, morality, and Bible doctrine. We discussed the atonement, God's sovereignty, election, and Providence—it was great! I have no memory of a father so I wanted to spend as much time with my son as I possibly could.

Our home in Heber Springs is about a mile from Greer's Ferry Lake. We had a pontoon boat, and I had a reputation as a great water skiing instructor! Never mind that I had never been on skies myself! I taught all my nephews and nieces to ski. Josh learned to ski when he was six years old. What was an even greater accomplishment was that I taught Glenda to drive the boat! Our most memorable vacation was not the year we went to Disney World, or the Rocky Mountains, or white-water rafting down the Colorado River. No! It was the time we stayed home and spent the entire week on the lake—fishing, skiing, riding the tornado tube, grilling hamburgers and hot dogs, or jumping off the bluffs with friends. Our Lord smiled on us—we were blessed indeed!

Glenda, Josh nor I thought of me as being handicapped. We often laughed until our sides hurt at the way others responded to me. Once, while attending the Southern Baptist Convention in Dallas, a man kept staring at me. Finally, he walked right up close and interrupted us. He did not introduce himself; he just looked me over and asked, "MS?" I said, "No, MDM." He said, "I've never heard of that." I replied, "Milton David Miller!" I thought I had inspiration on that one. After coming to church thirty minutes early to watch Glenda help me up the front steps, some older ladies from Tuscumbia, Alabama, sent word via the pastor to say, "That if I would rub *Icy Hot* on my legs, I would be good as new within a week!"

How God Used Suffering to Rescue Our Son

Josh was saved at age fifteen. He made much progress in sanctification. He was faithful in church, tithed, and read his Bible daily. All was well. Josh grew to be 6 feet, 7 inches tall and weighed 220 pounds. He was a pole vaulter on a state championship team. Glenda and I were extremely proud of him. We prayed with him and for him daily. We were confident that Josh was prepared spiritually, emotionally and theologically to do well in college. We had a "million" conversations with him regarding temptation being greater when you are away from home. He was ready.

When Josh went off to college, he went with three of the finest young men from our town. They were from great families. The four of them had an apartment together. Life was good. Josh came home every weekend. However, in their second semester, they began to drink and goof-off. I would have bet my retirement income that Josh would never have done that. We had a "million" conversations regarding alcoholic beverages. He had practically memorized my sermon on "Rechabite Religion" from Jeremiah 35. How could this have happened? Things got worse the second year. Glenda and I knew he had backslidden, but we were oblivious to his drinking. Josh did not want to go back to school after two years. Our dreams for him were being shattered before our eyes, and we were helpless to do anything about it. When we learned that he was drinking, we were devastated!

We tried to intervene, but things got worse. We wept and prayed. We questioned ourselves. We humbled ourselves. We resolved to do all we could to help. We shared our burden with godly friends. Our church family prayed for Josh. Some of the brethren encouraged Josh to repent, but he was unmoved by their admonitions.

Before long, Josh announced that his girlfriend, Ashley, was pregnant, and they would be getting married soon. Within eighteen months, they were married, became parents, and then divorced. Our hearts were sorely grieved for Josh. It is a parents' nightmare to see your son self-destruct. To say that Josh was out of the will of God is to state the obvious. He was miserable. We assured him of our love and that "the Lord can restore what the cankerworm hath devoured."

Just when you think things cannot get any worse, often they do. On August 1, 2003, Josh and I spent the afternoon together working on a hunting spot near our home. I needed a spot that was wheelchair-accessible for me. Little did either of us know that would be the last time I would ever see Josh stand or walk. The next time he and I visited that spot, both of us would be in wheelchairs. The next day, Glenda and I went to Memphis, where I was scheduled to preach in three churches over the following ten days. At 4:00 a.m. we were awakened by a call from a friend of Josh. He told us that Josh had been in a terrible auto accident and had been transported from the scene by helicopter to St. Vincent's Hospital in Little Rock, Arkansas. All we could learn from the call is that it was really serious, and we should come immediately.

Is he alive? What will we find when we arrive? Will Glenda be able to drive this 40-foot motor home the 130 miles to Little Rock? We prayed and thanked our God that Josh was in His hands. We arrived at the hospital at 7:30 a.m. on the Lord's Day morning to discover that Josh had sustained injuries to his liver, lungs, colon, shoulder, and that he had completely severed the C–5 level of his spinal cord. If he lived, he would be quadriplegic. He was in a coma. Life and death hung in the balance. We were stunned and exhausted. Our Christianity was experiencing a reality check.

Josh did live! He is quadriplegic. He was in the hospital four and a half months. He had five surgeries and was nauseated every day for four months. He was on a ventilator for nine weeks, had a J-Juneau, and an eleostomy, and lost 100 pounds.

How could this have happened to us? How strange that in a family of three, two of us are in wheelchairs. Where was God in all of this? Why do the righteous suffer? If God loves us, why has He allowed this to happen? If God was in control, why didn't He do something? The child of God who has never been forced by circumstances to wrestle with these tough questions is a rare and extremely blessed individual.

Instead of majoring on these questions, we have chosen rather to acknowledge the Providence of God in all of this. For example, our Lord did not allow our son to die. All who worked the accident scene said he would not live. He was thrown 60 feet from the vehicle into a tree, but God kept him alive. His intellect and personality are intact. Praise the Lord! If they had asked us, we would have gone to the Baptist Medical Center rather than the Roman Catholic hospital. We are Baptists and Baptist Hospital gives ordained Baptist preachers a discount, and Josh had no insurance. Baptist Medical Center ER was filled, so Providence arranged for us to meet "angels unawares" at the Catholic hospital. The second day there, an attractive lady approached us with a gift bag for Glenda. It was Marilyn Mansfield, the CEO's wife. She said a mutual friend had called to tell her about Josh, and she wanted to meet him and pray for him. She assured us that Josh would have the finest care possible.

Mrs. Mansfield asked if we would go to the ICU with her. Although it was not a scheduled visitation time, we assumed the CEO's wife could get us in to see our son. When we entered the room, this dear lady took Josh's hand in hers and began to sing, "When peace like a river attendeth my way, when sorrows like sea billows roll—whatever my lot, thou hast taught me to say, It is well, it is well with my soul." The next day she called to say she was bringing us a "home-cooked" meal for dinner. It was a roast with potatoes, carrots and onions. There were green beans, creamed corn, cornbread and fried okra—which thing my soul loveth!

A couple of days later, Mrs. Mansfield called and asked us to meet her in a particular room at 1:00 p.m. because the hospital choir wanted to present a private concert of gospel music for Glenda and me. As soon as we arrived, thirty-five saints stood and commenced singing old time southern gospel favorites. It was wonderful. Afterwards, they prayed for Josh and wept with us. One dear lady asked if she could clean Josh's feet. The human body sheds its dead skin by our movement throughout the day. However, when you lie motionless for days, dead skin builds up on your cuticles and between the toes. This precious soul poured oil on her bare hands and began to clean Josh's feet. As she cleaned, she sang, "There is a fountain filled with blood, drawn from Emmanuel's veins, and sinners plunged beneath that flood loose all their guilty stains." This is Providence!

Our Lord did not allow our son to go to the judgment backslidden. This is grace. After Josh regained consciousness, he was finally able to whisper a bit. He motioned with his eyes for us to come close. We gathered as close to him as possible and listened intently as he whispered, "I have been talking to God, and He has forgiven me of my sins. I want to ask my family now to forgive me of my sins." Of course, we forgave him and assured him of our love for him. I said to his mother as we left his room that day: "If God is pleased to take our son in death today, the bitterness of his death will have been sweetened by the knowledge of his repentance." His repentance has deepened, and his renewal continues. Praise the Lord!

Providence did not allow Josh to be overcome with depression. After a month at the hospital, we were told that Josh was in clinical depression and needed more anti-depression medicine and that we should have the hospital psychologist visit him. They said he will be angry and bitter. Glenda and I did not think he was angry or depressed. We thought he was handling things with dignity and grace. He clearly understood that God had not dealt with him after his iniquity, and he was profoundly grateful for such mercy. So, we steadfastly resisted giving Josh more anti-depressants or psychological counseling.

A few days later, the psychologist approached me in the cafeteria. She said she understood I was Josh Miller's father. She wanted to ask permission to visit him—she had been informed that he was terribly depressed. She was nice and she was kind. I thanked her for her interest and inquired of her education. With tongue-in-cheek, I told her that I was a country preacher and had a natural aversion toward psychology and psychiatry. However, if we decided Josh needed psychological counseling, we felt comfortable with her.

When Glenda and I arrived at the ICU, Josh was feeling better. He said, "Dad, you know what I want us to do the first week I'm home?" I said, "What?" He answered, "I want us to go to the deer camp." My heart sank! I could hardly control my emotions as I thought, "Josh may never go to the deer camp again." I didn't know what to say. At last I said, "Josh, we can't do that. You don't realize how fragile you are. It may be months before you are able to do that." Josh protested, "Ah, we can do it—we can do it." I said, "Where will we sleep? We only have one bedroom in the cabin. Which one of us will sleep in the loft?" Josh smiled and said, "You and I can sleep in the same bed—we will lay there like two mummies!" As we all laughed,

I said to Glenda, "Go get that psychologist. This will blow her right out of the saddle!" Instead of being depressed, Josh became a source of joy and spiritual encouragement to his family, friends and the hospital staff! Praise the Lord!

Providence knew more than we did. When they told us that Josh would be able to go home, I begged them to keep him longer! I was so afraid we could not care for him adequately. I told them I would sell the farm! I would cash in my retirement account—whatever I had to do to pay for another four to six weeks of care at the hospital. How would Glenda endure taking care of Josh and me? The most fearful day of my life was the day we brought Josh home. Josh was 6 feet, 7 inches tall and weighed 120 pounds. We had an oxygen machine, feeding tube, catheter, elieostomy, two decubedous sores exposing the bone, unending nausea, and more medicines than a pharmacist could manage. How would we possibly manage all of this? I will tell you how. Our Lord surrounded us with an army of family, friends, assistants, nurses and doctors who came to our aid. Our church provided meals for us for eighteen months. We had helpers who stayed with us round the clock. Hundreds of churches prayed for us. All of our financial needs were met according to "His riches in glory by Christ Jesus." Praise the Lord!

We came home on Friday afternoon. On Saturday and Sunday Josh was nauseated and could not attempt to eat. How could he not eat and sustain life? Even the feeding tube made him sick. We bribed, begged, cajoled; we even threatened—to no avail. On Monday morning, he was nauseated between 7:00 and 7:30. I prayed and prayed. At 11:00 a.m. I was alone with Josh and he said, "You are not going to believe this, but I'm hungry. Do you suppose Mom has anything I can eat?" When I could get over the initial shock I said, "It just happens that Mom has a pot of homemade beef stew on the stove, and I will have her bring you some." When Glenda and I could stop crying and rejoicing, she prepared a bowl of stew and brought it to Josh's room. He loved it. I kept waiting for him to be nauseated, but he finished the stew without a problem—we could hardly believe it! About thirty minutes later, Josh asked for more stew. His mother brought him the second bowl of stew with crackers. Our God flipped a switch somewhere, and Josh has not been nauseated since. Praise the Lord!

As God has brought us through this journey in Providence, much of my pain has been watching Glenda suffer. She has such a tremendous servant's heart. She loves her son so much she practically sacrificed herself to help him get well. She debunked the notion that you cannot go without sleep. She completely exhausted herself. Nothing but grace has sustained her. It was not until recently that she has regained her strength.

We have much for which to be thankful. Today—four and a half years later—Josh, though quadriplegic, is healthy. He weighs 190 pounds. He is a great father to our five year old grandson, Malachi. He teaches a Bible class at his church. He is a full-time student and plans to attend law school. He serves on the Governor's Commission for the Disabled and is a very competitive deer hunter. In fact, he recently harvested a nine-point and an eight-point buck with one shot from a crossbow. Josh and I both cherish our time together teaching Malachi how to hunt. We are blessed.

6

Listening to the Silence

Danny Blair

When I was invited to share from my experience as a Christian minister married to a deaf lady, my first thought was, "Why me? We don't suffer because of my wife's deafness." But as I pondered the fact that both society and church generally associate deafness with tragedy, loss and suffering, I concluded that this association—fair or not—has profoundly influenced my personal experience as a follower of Christ and as a minister of His gospel. In fact, looking back over the past twenty years, widespread lack of awareness and misunderstanding regarding deaf people may be the single most cogent reason for my continued involvement in deaf ministry and education. As one noted politician exclaimed during the "Deaf President Now" protest at Gallaudet University in 1988, "The problem is not that the students do not hear; the problem is that the hearing world does not listen."[1] I invite you now to "listen" to our story, a lone stanza written into the collective epic of those who live in silence.

Deafness as Suffering

To begin, it is incorrect to assume that deaf people suffer from their deafness just as it is naïve to think we all know what we are talking about when we use the word "suffering." In a broad sense, as Hauerwas put it,

---

[1] Harlan Lane, Robert Hoffmeister, and Ben Bahan, *Journey into the DEAF-WORLD* (San Diego: DawnSign Press, 1996), 130.

"Suffering has as its root sense the idea of submitting or being forced to submit to and endure some particular set of circumstances."[2] Thus life itself may be viewed as something we suffer, our incessant survival from cradle to grave, culminating in the ultimate suffering of death. But this sort of all-encompassing philosophical description stops short of the general, instinctive impression that suffering involves the experience of pain, grief, stress, loss, or threat of imminent danger. In terms of medical evaluation, suffering is something to be treated and cured if possible; and in this particular sense, many deaf people resist the uncritical assumption that deafness equals suffering.

Accordingly, it is this perception of "poor pitiful deaf people" that galls deaf people, many of whom are quite content and genuinely happy with their deafness, especially those who are born deaf or became deafened early in life.[3] This is not to say that they do not require certain accommodations to function within a predominantly hearing society, nor is it to deny that most deaf people experience a lifetime of challenges, including disabling social structures and outright discrimination. In this regard, yes, of course deaf people suffer. Constant social oppression, communication barriers and interpersonal isolation can be expected to trigger psychological and emotional distress in anyone, deaf or hearing. But these forces are external environmental factors, not the direct result of hearing impairment.

In the field of Deaf Studies it is critical to distinguish between *impairment*, which involves a pathological medical condition of an individual, and *disability*, which is a social construction rooted in the surrounding environment. With this distinction in place, it follows that if there is a categorical "suffering" of deaf people, it does not stem directly from the individual's lack of hearing as, for example, physical pain stems from cancer. Most deaf-related problems derive from society's inability to accommodate the difference in communication modalities, namely, visual instead of aural. If proof is needed for this assertion, try dropping a hearing person who is unfamiliar with American Sign Language (ASL) into a room full of deaf people: the hearing person may soon change his opinion about the "disability" of the deaf people when he discovers that it is he who is "signing impaired" and, hence, disabled with regard to communication. I enact

---

[2] Stanley Hauerwas, *Suffering Presence: Theological Reflections on Medicine, the Mentally Handicapped, and the Church* (Notre Dame, IN: University of Notre Dame Press, 1986), 28.

[3] In cases of postlingual deafness and late-deafened adults, hearing loss is often accompanied by intense loss, grief and suffering. People who are born deaf often report no sense of loss or sorrow because they have no recall of experience with hearing.

this scenario regularly with my ASL students and they immediately get the point!

Yet through these and other common experiences, most notably a shared language, many deaf people find the footing of a socio-linguistic community. This sense of "deaf community" enhances personal and social identity, which in turn provides a platform for political, social and economic solidarity and activism similar to ongoing civil rights efforts of ethnic minorities, women and people with disabilities. Ultimately, as deaf people gain accessibility into prominent structures of society, including education, politics, economics, arts and entertainment, not to mention religion, their likelihood of leading a relatively "happy" life increases proportionately.

Welcome to the DEAF-WORLD [4]

Believe it or not, I did not set out as a young man or even as a young minister to become a professor of ASL or a minister with deaf people. The thought had never entered my mind until I was thirty, at which time I honestly believe it was placed directly in my lap by the Lord. To which I might add that I find great comfort in knowing that "The heart of man plans his way, but the Lord directs his steps" (Proverbs 16:9, NIV).

My first exposure to the DEAF-WORLD came when I was the pastor of a semi-rural, central Alabama church in 1989. At the end of a typical Sunday morning service, to my delight, a threesome of a married, twenty-something deaf couple and their interpreter made their way to the front of the church to greet the pastor. This rite of "walking the aisle," according to this church, usually indicated a desire to make a public profession of faith in Christ. Or it could mean the person sought baptism, church membership, or perhaps to ask for special prayer, counseling, or some other assistance. In their case, the interpreter, Jan, was already a member of our church. Danny and Tammy, the deaf couple, were seeking membership.

"Wonderful," came my heartfelt response to their request, followed by the superbly intelligent recognition, "Uh...how do we communicate?" After a moment of chuckling at my ignorance, I asked Jan if she might be willing to teach a basic sign language class for beginners, at which suggestion Danny smiled broadly and answered for her by signing a big "Yes!" As I copied his sign for "Yes," my very first sign as I recall, little did I realize that this was my first baby step into a lifelong journey into a new world!

That following Sunday evening, as promised, we started our very first sign language class. As it turned out, Jan was Danny's aunt and had learned

[4] This compound term is written with small caps and hyphenation to indicate an ASL literary gloss, a device used frequently in Deaf literature.

what I now call a home-grown dialect of ASL from Danny and Tammy and their friends. She was not a trained interpreter and had never taught a class on sign language, but she was keenly motivated by her desire to lead Danny and Tammy to faith in Christ through involvement with our church. So like the lad who offered all he had—a few loaves and fishes—in service to the Lord, she hauled out her books and videos and began zealously sharing her skills with 20–25 novices, myself included. Interestingly, at least half of our class was comprised of local community residents who had not previously attended our church, several of whom later joined thanks to what they had witnessed in sign language class.

As the weeks rolled by, our class dwindled to perhaps a dozen students that were at least somewhat committed to learning or otherwise fascinated with the deaf scene. Within a month several of us were beginning to catch on, having mastered our letters (manual ABCs) and some basic vocabulary. Jan led the classes, while Danny and Tammy helped us practice (the key to learning ASL—practice, practice, practice). Then came a personal watershed that decisively drew me into the DEAF-WORLD, not exactly a Damascus road experience, but impressive enough to change my life. You guessed it—a woman appeared—a beautiful, winsome, courageous, deaf woman named Angela.

It happened like this. One Sunday evening, maybe the third or fourth week of our sign language class, we had some deaf visitors named Angela and Rocky. They were friends of Danny and Tammy, and I think we all assumed they were dating, engaged, or otherwise mutually "spoken for." Angela and Rocky stayed around for the sign language class, chiming in with encouragement and a good bit of humor, making it an unusually enjoyable session, then they left afterwards with Danny and Tammy. "Nice couple," I thought, not really expecting to see them again although we had emphatically invited them back.

That following Sunday morning, sure enough, who showed up for church? It was Angela. Although she had been baptized as a teenager, she had expressed interest in attending our church because we now had an interpreter, something she had frequently missed in her previous experience with churches. At the conclusion of the service, she came by to sign "Hello" and to thank me for the message, at which point I inquired about Rocky. "Where's Rocky?" I asked, this time in slow, kindergarten-ish sign language. "Oh, I don't know," she shrugged, "we're old friends but I don't keep up with him." At this point in the conversation, matchmaker Tammy, with her bow drawn and aimed, jumped in, signing, "Angela's coming over to watch the game tonight (Alabama football); would you like to join us?" Modest and reserved person that I am, I had to think about it—for about two seconds. "Well, if you insist," and I accepted the invitation. I cannot even remember Alabama's opponent that evening (and I am a rabid University of Alabama alumnus), but I clearly remember asking Angela if she might be so kind as to "tutor" me in sign language—over dinner, I might add. She accepted and, to significantly shorten this part of our story, she is now my wife of nearly twenty years.

A Conspicuous Need for Deaf Missions

During the first three to six months of our sign language class, we began to sense that our church needed to establish a distinct ministry focused on outreach and pastoral care for the deaf in our area. Our church was located about twenty miles from Alabama School for the Deaf (ASD) in Talladega, and since starting the sign language class, several new deaf friends had visited our church. So it seemed that providence was leading us into a full-blown deaf ministry, though we scarcely knew what that was.

Another factor that underscored the need was the sheer lack of a ministry for the deaf in our community. With ASD just down the road and a significant number of deaf people living within that twenty-mile radius, we initially assumed deaf ministries would be everywhere. But as we began calling local churches in search of advice and possible collaboration, we were surprised to find hardly any active ministries for deaf people. In fact, we found only one in the entire region, located in Talladega near ASD, a thirty-minute commute from our town. Several local churches advertised in the Yellow Pages (this was before the explosion of the Internet) that they provided interpreters for the deaf. But when we called for more information the responses ranged from, "Oh, I didn't know we had an interpreter" to "Let me check on that and get back to you." With each call we gained a clearer picture: There we were in the very buckle of the "Bible belt," only a half-hour from ASD, yet the gospel of free grace had scarcely penetrated the DEAF-WORLD.

If God used my relationship with Angela to draw me into the DEAF-WORLD, it is the reality of this virtually unreached, unevangelized linguistic minority that keeps me here. When viewed as a linguistic people group, deaf people comprise a trans-cultural, trans-geographical population numbering hundreds of millions.[5] In biblical terms, deaf people saturate "every nation, tribe, people and language" (Revelation 7:9, HCSB); so when Jesus commands us to go to the nations, He surely has deaf people in mind.

---

[5] Although many deaf ethnicities have their own distinct sign languages (e.g. Japanese Sign Language, Mexican Sign Language, Russian Sign Language, etc.), cross-cultural and inter-linguistic communication is generally more prompt and natural than communication between two audibly spoken languages.

Interestingly, while writing this chapter I received an email from a local pastor here in Southern California, entitled "IMB [International Mission Board of the Southern Baptist Convention] isn't deaf anymore!" In the note my friend pointed out that "IMB has finally realized that the deaf are the largest unreached people group in the world."[6] As a teacher/preacher, I love to see the lights go on in the minds of students and worshipers as they grasp some new truth and cry "Eureka!" And how much more when an agency with such incredible potential as IMB finally gets it!

Resistance to Difference

Yet it was at this juncture, when the light of the gospel began to shine into the hearts of a few deaf souls, that opposition began to manifest itself. Approximately six months after Danny, Tammy and Angela began attending our church, it became clear that in spite of their varying individual experiences in religion, they had never been united with Christ through regeneration and conversion. Accordingly, upon their profession of union with Christ, I had the privilege of baptizing all three of them in a single, memorable service. And for a while, it seemed like an effectual door had indeed been opened by God.

Soon after Danny, Tammy and Angela were baptized, others followed and our church began to grow, but not to the delight of all. In addition to new believers being added to our membership, we were also redesigning our Christian educational program, bolstering our deacon ministry, and renovating our facilities. And we were assimilating the deaf members into all that we did. Then one Sunday morning just as I was about to go onto the platform to begin the service, I was stopped at the door by a matriarch of the church whose family had been instrumental in the establishment of the church some 35–40 years prior.

"Brother Danny," she began in her refined southern drawl, "This is our church," clearly indicating her disapproval of the changes accompanying the recent growth of the church in general, and as I would later find out at the meeting of elders and deacons, the deaf ministry in particular. Some of the old guard—few in number but what you might call the internal or informal power structure of the church—had concluded that my priorities had become misplaced. One dear brother (I call him "dear" in utmost sincerity) even suggested that in my zeal to include the deaf, I had perhaps

[6] For statistical research on the Deaf as an unevangelized people group, see www.peoplegroups.org. Even in the US, church growth demographers estimate that only about 1 percent of the 2–3 million ASL users have been evangelized in their primary language.

become obsessed with them. The fact that I was now dating Angela did nothing to refute his suggestion. At any rate, it seems that just as the deaf were being baptized into the faith, our ministry was likewise being initiated into the subtle oppression that insidiously defines the experience of being deaf.

Another defining incident occurred when our church hosted its annual Bible conference. With several of my dearest friends and fellow pastors as keynote speakers, the Biblical emphasis as always was on the sovereignty of God in salvation. There was expository preaching on the great themes of divine election, effectual calling, particular redemption, perseverance of the saints, and the fall and depravity of mankind. Since my earliest days as a follower of Jesus Christ (mid-1970s) I have cherished theses truths known as historic Calvinism, and at this time I was doing my best to faithfully lead our Baptist church, including the new deaf believers, into this doctrinal tradition.

But as anyone remotely familiar with ASL knows, the process of translating specialized language like theology from English to ASL is not automatic. It is tedious and requires time and ingenuity. So when one of the conference speakers, a close friend of mine, began to quiz Angela about her belief in predestination and election (concepts with which well-trained pastors and theologians inevitably struggle), she apparently failed to articulate her belief to his satisfaction.

This will come as no surprise if we realize that there simply are no commonly recognized visual cognates (signs) for terms like election, atonement, justification, sanctification, regeneration, predestination, redemption and many others. Nonetheless, upon seeing that Angela could not express her faith in what to him were the acceptable terms, my friend expressed his sincere doubts about the authenticity of her conversion. He insinuated that at best I had ignorantly veered from the truth, or at worst that I had knowingly sold out my faith and conscience for a woman. God willing, time and eternity will prove that I did neither. Yet, my point in mentioning this is not self-vindication, but to offer an insight into the relational and spiritual injustices suffered by deaf people even among loving believers through sheer misunderstanding.

Another painful instance of misunderstanding (suffering?) that resulted in a broken friendship (loss?) occurred more directly in connection with my marriage to Angela. I will never forget the sound of disbelief in the voice of my friend—a successful bank executive, a zealous partner in ministry, and a member our church—when I told her that I had decided to marry Angela. True, I had only known Angela for a little over a year, but during that year our relationship had transformed both of our lives. Angela had come to a saving knowledge of the Lord Jesus Christ through the instrumentality of my preaching ministry—glory to God! I had discovered a world of 20 million people like her in desperate need of having the gospel message translated into their own language. Nevertheless, it was inconceivable to my friend that I, a 31-year-old hearing pastor with promising ministry opportunities, should marry a deaf person. When I asked my friend why she was shocked at my decision (I had expected congratulations and best wishes that typically accompany engagement announcements), she groped for words until finally blurting out, "If I have to explain it to you, I guess there's no point!"

Needless to say, my friend's seemingly judgmental attitude created a significant rift in our friendship and in our ministry partnership. Yet through the years—almost twenty since my engagement to Angela—this saying of my friend has haunted me, partly because of the broken fellowship and partly because of the accuracy of her prediction. At first, I viewed her incredulity as some knee-jerk reaction to her previously unexposed prejudice. It is similar to that of certain white people who imagine they are not racist until the black couple moves in next door. I scarcely dignified her insult with more than "Thanks for your opinion, goodbye."

Since then, looking back over the various stages of our marriage—the honeymoon, the birth of children, college and graduate studies, planting churches, cross-country career moves and the looming prospect of an empty nest—I have come to view my friend's admonishment, painful and perhaps tactless as it seemed at the time, as completely sane and well-intentioned. Without going into detail, let me say that there are reasons why 85–90 percent of the marriages between deaf and hearing people end in divorce.[7] While Angela and I are committed to finishing in that ten percent of marriages that survive and even flourish, we can testify that it is not easy—in our case, impossible without divine grace—to combine two languages, two cultures, two worlds into one family. This is especially true in the fishbowl existence of public ministry. But God is abundantly gracious. Because He has sustained us through many trials, I want to close this chapter by outlining four transferrable principles that have been spiritual points of growth for me along the way.

Reflections along the Way

First, God calls us into the suffering of others, whether physical, bodily affliction or social oppression and discrimination, in order to bring His

---

[7] Statistics from Gallaudet Research Center, Gallaudet University.

love into their lives. Perhaps nothing characterizes the ministry of Jesus more than Hebrews 2:9–10, which says:

> But we do see Jesus—made lower than the angels for a short time so that by God's grace He might taste death for everyone—crowned with glory and honor because of the suffering of death. For it was fitting in bringing many sons to glory, that He, for whom and through whom all things exist, should make the source of their salvation perfect through sufferings (HCSB).

As we follow Jesus, we should expect that He will lead us into frequent contact and intimate fellowship with anguish and suffering, not only as a comfort to those who are in need but as means of fashioning us into His image.

Second, inclusion of those who are "different" will likely incur opposition. From the beginning of His earthly ministry until His final triumphant breath on the cross, Jesus Christ was misunderstood, falsely characterized, and constantly slandered, largely because He habitually included those whom society had excluded. Wherever He preached, healed and served, He inevitably sought out public "sinners," women, Gentiles, the poor, the sick and the disabled to demonstrate both the universality and the particularity of His call to salvation. But His sovereign mercy was answered by ungrounded charges of gluttony, drunkenness, lawlessness, false prophecy, illegitimacy, and demon-possession. If we are truly His disciples, should we expect open arms and accolades for countering the same cosmos that crucified Him?

Third, as we enter into solidarity with those who suffer, whether through our own personal suffering or oppression, or through *koinonia* (intimate Christian fellowship), we and our faith communities are immeasurably enriched. Through my involvement in various deaf communities around the country (and increasingly in other countries), I have received insights and understanding, love and fellowship, not to mention challenges and "growth opportunities," that I could never have experienced any other way. Further, as Angela and I have been enabled to serve various churches, schools, conferences and organizations by raising awareness of the DEAF-WORLD, inevitably faces light up and tears flow as believers call to mind neighbors, co-workers, students, and even relatives that have been unintentionally ignored. They have been excluded because of a disability, a sickness or disease, a broken marriage, or lost job. As barriers are replaced by bridges, the words of our Lord take on fresh meaning: "Those who are well do not need a doctor, but the sick do" (Matthew 9:12, HCSB).

Fourth, we are "called" to follow Jesus, not our perceived vocation, career, or profession. To illustrate this odd-sounding assertion, let me relate another personal story. As a student at Beeson Divinity School in 1994, I had the privilege of coordinating an Evangelism Leadership Seminar led by Leighton Ford. During one of the class sessions, Dr. Ford asked the students, fifteen from Beeson and approximately fifteen international students from as far as China and New Zealand, to go around the oblong conference table sharing our sense of "calling." Obediently we followed suit: "preacher," said one, "missionary," said another; a few gave more entrepreneurial descriptions—business or para-church leader—and one or two were undecided. At the time, my answer was "pastor/evangelist" or "church planter."

After we had gone full circle, I waited patiently for Dr. Ford's personal "calling," which I thought was a no-brainer—he was an evangelist after the order of his brother-in-law-Billy Graham! But his answer, surprising on one hand, yet entirely predictable on the other, was to become one of the most formative moments of my life: "My calling is to follow Jesus," he started, "and the directions He takes sometimes change. Earlier in life, He led me into evangelism; now I believe He is leading me to mentor others through teaching and writing."

Over a decade later, I can affirm that the Lord's path sometimes makes unexpected turns. At times I have wondered, "Deaf ministry? Professor of American Sign Language? Southern California? Whose life am I living? I thought I was a country preacher from Kentucky?" But the one constant has been and still is my Shepherd's voice, saying, "Follow me!" And by His infinite grace and eternal love, I am still listening. To God be all the glory!

7

Serving God through the Storm

Fred Luter

Franklin Avenue Baptist Church, located in New Orleans, Louisiana, was on the brink of making a tremendous impact for the Kingdom of God. We were having five Sunday morning worship services (including a youth and children service) at our main campus. Plus, we were having another service at a satellite location eight miles away in east New Orleans to accommodate our membership of over 7,000. Two months before Hurricane Katrina we had purchased ninety acres of property for future growth. The new property would allow us to build a 5,000 seat worship center, educational building, youth and children's building, an administrative wing, athletic fields, and something we never had at our inner-city location—parking, parking, parking!

Two weeks before the hurricane in all three of our main services we showed the membership a DVD of the vision we had planned for the ninety acres—the people stood and applauded. As another testimony of our growth, a week before the Hurricane, 351 couples were enjoying themselves at our annual Couples Retreat in Sandestin, Florida. The Lord was truly blessing our ministry beyond what we had ever thought or imagined. And then Katrina showed up, and she changed our lives forever.

Hurricane Katrina

My wife, Elizabeth, and I grew up in the Lower Ninth Ward in the City of New Orleans. Both of us went through Hurricane Betsy forty years ago when the Lower Ninth Ward was flooded. Because of this prior experience, we did not hesitate when the mayor of New Orleans gave the order to evacuate for Hurricane Katrina. We left our home, church and city on the Saturday before the hurricane hit. We really thought we would be gone no more than two days like most times when we had to leave the city. The year before, for Hurricane Ivan, we evacuated to Dallas, where our son Chip was a student at Dallas Baptist University. This time we decided to spend two days with our daughter Kimberly in Birmingham, where she is a fifth grade math and science teacher.

As all America now knows, those two days turned out to be seven months. When the levees broke during the hurricane 80 percent of our city was flooded. My home received five feet of water, and the church where I have been pastor for nineteen years received nine feet of water. The ninety acres we had purchased was covered with twelve feet of water! Our city had just gone through the most devastating hurricane in the history of our nation. As a result of the flood waters over 1,000 people, including two local pastors, lost their lives.

Where Do We Go from Here?

About two weeks after the flood I was invited by Bobby Welch, the president of the Southern Baptist Convention, and David Hankins, the executive director of the Louisiana Baptist Convention, to view the city by helicopter. During that ride we were able to fly over the Franklin Avenue Baptist Church.

Tears began to fall as I looked down at our beloved sanctuary and family life center surrounded by the waters of Katrina. I will never forget asking myself the question in that helicopter: where do we go from here? Elizabeth and I began to get phone calls from our members who had been displaced all over America. My pastor friends from across the country were also calling with invitations to preach in their pulpits since I no longer had a church where I could preach. From September through December, my wife and I traveled all over this country preaching in different churches. Everywhere we went we saw the displaced members of our church. By God's grace and some dear men of God, I did not miss one Sunday preaching after Katrina.

One Church in Three Cities!

While living with our daughter in Birmingham, Elizabeth and I started making plans to travel to three cities for Sunday worship services. Three churches had agreed to allow us to have worship in their buildings: First

Baptist Church in Houston, Texas; First Baptist Church in New Orleans, Louisiana.; and the Istrouma Baptist Church in Baton Rouge, Louisiana. Every first and third Saturday of the month, we would drive the five hours from Birmingham to New Orleans. We would pray that we would have a place to stay each night. We would try to get a few hours sleep, and then get up Sunday morning for a 7:30 a.m. service at First Baptist. We would then drive for an hour to Baton Rouge for a 1:00 p.m. service at Istrouma Baptist Church. Depending on what I had scheduled on Monday, we would spend the night in Baton Rouge and drive back to Birmingham on Monday morning.

On the second and fourth Saturdays we would drive eleven hours from Birmingham to Houston for a 1:00 p.m. service at Houston's First Baptist Church on Sunday. I will never forget the amusing dialogue that Elizabeth and I had when we were leaving Houston the Monday morning after the fourth Sunday. As we were packing our Jeep Cherokee for our drive back to Birmingham I looked at the love of my life and the apple of my eye and asked her a question: "Do you think we can do this the rest of the year?" My "prime rib" of twenty-five wonderful years looked me straight in the eyes and said, "I think you can do this the rest of the year!" During our eleven hour drive back to Birmingham, I had to constantly remind her of the vows we took on November 11, 1980, particularly "for better or for worse"(smile).

Around July 2006, more New Orleanians were returning back home. This included Elizabeth and me. We then began holding services every Sunday in New Orleans. I could not continue the twice monthly trip to Houston. My assistant pastor, Sam Young, had been with me sixteen of the nineteen years I was at Franklin Avenue Church. He moved from Memphis to Houston to oversee and pastor the Houston church. Gary Mack, Pastor of Family Life, helped start and maintain the church in Houston. He then moved back to New Orleans to help us meet the growing counseling needs from those members suffering from Katrina stress syndrome. At the beginning of 2007 more of our members moved back to New Orleans. We then moved our Baton Rouge service to Florida Boulevard Baptist Church, where we still meet.

The Church Is Alive and Well

The past three years have been the most difficult days of my life. Hurricane Katrina affected my faith like nothing in my Christian life has before. However, God has used this journey to convince me that His grace is sufficient! Even though our physical church building on Franklin Avenue was destroyed by this devastating hurricane, God's church is *alive and well* in New Orleans, Baton Rouge and Houston. In April 2008 we plan to move back into our renovated sanctuary.[1] I do not believe that God has brought us this far just to leave us. With all that we have gone through, we are determined to *serve God through the storm!*

Lessons Learned from the Storm

As I travel across the country I am often asked the question, "What lessons have you learned from Hurricane Katrina?" Well, I have learned a number of lessons from this storm. During the time of any trial or setback in life, we as believers often have questions. And believe me, I had a *lot* of questions for God. Like the questions I have asked God since Hurricane Katrina. I could not understand why my church was flooded. Why were other churches flooded? Why was New Orleans Baptist Theological Seminary flooded? Why was Xavier University flooded? Why was Dillard University flooded? Why were Tulane University and Loyola University flooded? However Bourbon Street, the city's famous tourist attraction, filled with bars and strip clubs, was high and dry! As a matter of fact, it was the first time in the history of Bourbon Street that it was dry! I had many questions for God.

During my search for answers, like many believers, I began a serious search of God's Word. And also like many believers suffering lost and uncertainty, I began reading the book of Job. Think about it, if anyone could understand and make sense of my plight, I have no doubt it was Job. If there was anyone that could relate to what I was dealing with, it was Job. Think about it, brothers and sisters—Job is well known:

Not because he was a great author;
Not because he was a great military warrior;
Not because he killed a lion or bear with his bare hands;
Not because he built a historic city;
Not because he was a great missionary;
Not because he was a major prophet;
Not because he killed a giant with a sling shot and some rocks;
Not because he was an apostle of Jesus Christ;
Not because he was a great preacher;
Not because he was a great motivational speaker;

---

[1] The Franklin Avenue Baptist Church has since successfully moved back into a completely rebuilt and refurbished sanctuary.

No, No, a thousand times *No!* The only reason why Job is well known is because he *passed a great test!* That's it! Period! End of the story! Job is only well known because he passed a great test. Think about it. If Job had not passed a great test, his name would be pronounced "job!"

A test is an examination; a test is a trial; a test is something that tries our trust. A test is something that tries our confidence. A test is something that tries our loyalty. A test is something that tries our allegiance. A test is something that tries our faith. Anybody can talk about faith. Anybody can sing about faith. Anybody can write about faith. Anybody can teach about faith. Anybody can preach about faith. But every now and then, like the three Hebrew boys in the book of Daniel, our faith is tried in the fire! And if anyone can relate to their faith being tried in the fire, no doubt it is Job, because in one day Job lost his health, his wealth, and his family. However Job passed the test by proclaiming, "though He slay me, yet I will trust Him" (Job 13:15).

So as I studied the life of Job, I wanted to know: how did he do it? How was Job able to hold on to his faith in spite of the fact that he lost his health, his wealth and his family? As if to add injury to insult, his wife turned her back on him. Well, there are three lessons that I learned from Job's ordeal. There are three things that Job taught me about life. These are the lessons I learned from the storm.

Lesson 1: God Pre-approves Every Test (Job 23:10a)

What Job did not realize during his trial was that in chapter one, God gave Satan permission to test Job. In other words, God *pre-approved* the test. Well, the lesson I learned from the storm is that there is nothing that a believer goes through that catches God by surprise. You and I may be surprised, but God is not surprised. Think about it, God was not surprised when Adam and Eve ate of the forbidden fruit. God was not surprised when Noah was laughed at as he built the Ark with no sign of rain in the sky. God was not surprised when Abraham and Sarah had a child in their old age (of course Abraham and Sarah was surprised!). God was not surprised when Joseph was betrayed by his brothers. God was not surprised when the children of Israel wandered forty years in the wilderness. God was not surprised when young David slew the giant Goliath. God was not surprised when Shadrach, Meshach, and Abednego were thrown into the fiery furnace. God was not surprised when Daniel was thrown into the lion's den. God was not surprised when Judas betrayed Jesus. God was not surprised when Peter denied Jesus. God was not surprised when Jesus hung, bled, and died on the cross for the sins of the world. No, none of these circumstances caught God by surprise because God pre-approved every test!

In like manner my friend, before Satan can put you through any trial or temptation God has to pre-approve the test. Even the test called Hurricane Katrina that destroyed the city of New Orleans. As with Job, Katrina did not catch God by surprise. God was not surprised when the levees broke. God was not surprised when my home flooded. God was not surprised when my church flooded. God was not surprised when the city flooded. No! God was not surprised by anything that happened as a result of Hurricane Katrina. God has a purpose in every trial. He put us on display before a watching world. Where is our hope? How would we respond to the disaster? Remember, Job says in the text that "God knows the way that I take." He knows who is ready and who is not. He knows who is going to pass the test and who will fail the test. He knows us and loves us, and He *pre-approves* every test.

Lesson 2: God Prepares Us for Every Test (Job 23:10b)

From the moment you and I became a child of God, from the moment you and I trusted Jesus Christ to save us, from the moment we became born-again believers, we knew God was at work. He works in every step of our lives and as we trust Him and follow Him. He prepares us for every test that comes our way throughout life.

Every time you read your Bible, He was preparing you.
Every time you said your prayers, He was preparing you.
Every time you went to Sunday school, He was preparing you.
Every time you went to Bible study, He was preparing you.
Every time you went to a worship service, He was preparing you.
Every time you heard a sermon, He was preparing you.
Every time you attended a revival, He was preparing you.
Every time you went on a fast, He was preparing you.
Every time the enemy attacked your body, He was preparing you.
Every time mess started in the ministry, He was preparing you.
Every time life has been unfair, He was preparing you.

And then, on top of all of that, here comes a disaster like Hurricane Katrina. However, God taught me that in the midst of the storm, if I would apply the promises and principles of His Word, I would come forth as pure gold! In other words, you will pass the test, because "this too shall pass!" And the reason it will pass is because God has prepared us for the test. Remember Romans 8:28 declares: "And we know that all things work together for good to those who love God, to those who are the called according to His purpose" (NKJV). The only reason some of us have not thrown in the towel yet is because God has prepared us for the test.

Lesson 3: God Preserves Us through Every Test (Job 23:11-12)

The only reason I am able to write this story today is because, in spite of all that I went through with Hurricane Katrina, God kept me!

Like Job, my feet held fast—He kept me!
Like Job, I kept His ways—He kept me!
Like Job, I did not turn aside—He kept me!
Like Job, I did not depart from His commandments—He kept me!
Like Job, I treasured His Words—He kept me!

In like manner, my brothers and sisters, if you stay committed to the way and the will of God, He will keep you through every test you face in life! It will not be easy, but God will preserve you through every test you face. Sometimes you may lose some material things. Sometimes you may cry. Sometimes you may continue to ask the question why. However, if you stay steadfast like Job, I have no doubt that your latter days will be better than your former days. And also like Job, because of your faithfulness, I truly believe that God will reward you double for your trouble! Therefore get ready for new opportunities. Get ready for new ministries. Get ready for more blessings. So, be encouraged my friends. God is at work! He is maturing us and fitting us to serve Him. By His grace and in His strength, you will weather the storm and pass the test.

8

God's Sufficient
And Abundant Grace

Michael Spradlin

A Process[1]

I was born in Columbus, Ohio, and raised in Little Rock, Arkansas, by great parents. I realized that something was missing in my life at the age of thirteen. Though it would be two years before I gave my life to Christ, the Lord sent several people into my life to share the gospel with me. At the invitation of some friends at school, I visited Sunset Lane Baptist Church in Little Rock, Arkansas, and heard Ed Edmondson preach about the need to make a personal commitment to Jesus Christ as Lord and Savior. So, as a fifteen year old, I gave my life to Christ following a Sunday evening service in February 1977. Repenting of my sins and accepting Jesus as Lord was the greatest event in my life and I will never get over it.

Within six months I sensed that the Lord was calling me to preach. At first I wrestled with a call to ministry because it did not fit into the plans that I had for my life. I finally came to a moment of surrender when I real-

---

[1] Spradlin uses Mulholland's definition of "Spiritual Formations" as the outline for his reflective essay. Robert Mulholland, *Invitation to a Journey* (InterVarsity Press, 1993), 15–17. Mulholland defines Spiritual Formation as: "Spiritual formation is the process of being conformed to the image of Christ by the gracious working of God's spirit, for the transformation of the world."

ized that I must follow whatever my Lord and Savior wanted me to do. I made my decision public as a sixteen year old and have never looked back. It is a sweet privilege to preach the gospel to people who need the Lord and to teach the Bible to people who love the Lord.

The advice I received from my pastor, Ed Edmondson, was to be enthusiastic and be a soul winner. One of the key moments in my spiritual formation was the advice from a family member to begin reading the Bible. In my mind "reading the Bible" meant starting at the beginning and reading straight through to the end. I began reading through the *Living Bible* and, even though it was a paraphrase, I was captivated by how the Lord had been at work for such a long time and in the lives of so many people.

In my later teenage years I momentarily doubted my salvation. I soon realized that my assessment of my own spiritual life was based more on my emotions than on my true spiritual state. It was an important time for me because I realized that I needed to be more concerned about the Lord's view of me than for my view of myself. I learned that passion and growth were separate from emotion and excitement. It was a great time spiritually.

Of Being Conformed to the Image of Christ

One Scripture mentioned over and over by my youth pastor, Craig Vire, was John the Baptist's statement about the Lord Jesus where he said, "I must decrease and he must increase" (John 3:30). This has always been a captivating thought in my spiritual development. I realized that dying to self is such a comprehensive statement. Dying to self relinquishes credit, ambition and so much more. Yet this self-sacrificial idea is the thought that has returned to my mind time and time again. It would be a pivotal verse in my spiritual journey to come.

In 1993, before moving to lead Mid-America Baptist Theological Seminary's Northeast Campus, I served for a year on faculty at the main campus in Memphis, Tennessee. I loved teaching at my alma mater and had never expected that I would one day return to be on faculty. In the winter of that year one of my former professors, T. V. Farris, died. He had struggled with health issues for years but had continued to preach and teach. At his funeral all of us on faculty served as honorary pallbearers, and it was the most powerful funeral service which I had ever attended. Months later, after moving to New York, I had a dream about Dr. Farris' funeral. In my dream I was sitting as a pallbearer in my academic gown and I was waiting for the service to start. I asked out loud what we were waiting for and someone sitting behind me said, "We are waiting for you." I realized that I was not ready and they told me that I needed to hurry. I awoke suddenly from this dream in a cold sweat. Though I have never taken this dream to be a message from the Lord (that is reserved for Scripture), I knew that I needed to step up my spiritual life. I was only going through the motions.

My wife Lee Ann and I had been married for thirteen years, had two sons, and had been through two miscarriages back-to-back when we found out that we were expecting again. To say that we were excited was an understatement. Our first son had been born while we were in Hughes, Arkansas, while I was on staff of the First Baptist Church. Our second son was born while we were church planters in Wichita, Kansas. Now it looked like our third child was due to arrive in New York. We had joked that our children were the only souvenirs that we could afford to take away from the places where we had lived.

Shortly after learning that a new addition to the family was due, our doctor told us that Lee Ann had a rare pregnancy complication that caused excessive hemorrhaging. This condition could eventually result in the loss of life to the mother or the baby. As often happens in times like this, we were in shock at first. Eventually, you realize that the Lord is in control and you strive for some semblance of normalcy. Unfortunately, normalcy was not to be in our immediate future.

Early one Sunday morning Lee Ann awakened me to let me know that she was having severe problems. I called a friend to come and stay with our boys as I rushed her to the hospital. There the doctor told us the news that the condition had erupted and that there was nothing that they could do to stop the bleeding except to abort the baby. Lee Ann stated that she would not consent to an abortion but that they could deliver the baby and then it would be in the Lord's hands. The doctor told us that he was on the ethics board at the hospital and that this was a legitimate time to abort the baby. The mother's life was in jeopardy and only the most extreme measures could save her life. The alternative was that both baby and mother would die. With Lee Ann's wishes known to the doctor, he told us that we had just a few minutes to change our minds. As sometimes happens with this condition, the bleeding stopped as suddenly as it had started.

Though relieved for the present, the long journey was not over. The bleeding continued off and on for the next several weeks. Our child was too young for the technology of the time to keep her alive if she were to be born. So, each day became a day on watch. Each hour was one of waiting and wondering—would this be the moment that we would be faced with the terrible decision yet again?

The doctors believed that it was time for Lee Ann to be checked into the hospital and placed on bed rest in the hopes that our baby could mature to the point of survivability. Not being very domesticated, this became a major handicap for me during the upcoming weeks. If our wonderful Trinity Baptist Church family (we had no family in the immediate area but did have some wonderful family help a few hours away) had not stepped in to help, I could not have made it.

Time slows down in periods of crisis such as this. I well remember one night carrying laundry upstairs and sitting down on the steps and telling myself "I quit." I am not sure to whom I thought I was offering my resignation. As I sat there I realized that our two sons needed me, that my wife lying in a hospital bed needed me, but that there was no more of me to go around. I thought about the promise that the Lord will never give you more than you can bear. I tried to let him know that I thought that I was past my limit. I realized that I could not handle the long days and lonely nights anymore. However, the thought occurred to me that if I couldn't handle a whole day, maybe, by God's grace I could last another hour. So I told myself that I would take things an hour at a time and if that became overwhelming then I would take things a few minutes at a time. Life sometimes boils down to its most basic elements. I knew the Lord still loved me because He promised. So when my bedridden, weakening wife asked me if I loved her I had my answer, "I promised." When my sons needed me, I knew that I would be there for them because I promised. I would not be the best Dad of all time but I would be there with them as their Dad. I would keep my word. The Lord kept His Word to me, so I must do the same.

Finally, the day arrived when the doctors wanted to bring our daughter into the world. We had witnessed to several of the hospital staff and knew that the Lord had used Lee Ann's illness to open doors for ministry. But this morning we felt a great weight of anxiety. Reading the Scripture and praying did not take that anxiety away. The moment of delivery had arrived. Our daughter was eight months along and had been receiving medication to prepare her for this day.

At first things began to go well in the delivery room. Laura, our new daughter, was born and seemed healthy, with just a few minor breathing problems. Moments later, one of the doctors said the fateful words, "Let's get Dad out of the room!" I saw Lee Ann groan and was soon ushered out. I began to make family calls to let all know that Laura had arrived. A call went out over the hospital intercom and I remember watching the nurses' station as two nurses began to look at me and weep. Lee Ann had been in her room for thirty straight days and had formed close ties with the wonderful nurses on the floor. One nurse came to me and told me that something had happened to my wife. I saw three medical staff with coolers of blood hurry to the operating room. Lee Ann's condition caused her to receive thirty-one units of blood that long day.

Soon a doctor came and told me that things were very serious but that they were doing all that they could. I told him that I knew it was a critical time, and he looked at me with his ashen face and said that it was much farther along than that. It is hard to imagine being alone in a hospital full of people but for a moment I was alone and empty. A familiar hymn came to mind and I sensed the Lord's closeness, but honestly, the anxiety was overwhelming. As I thought of my two boys and new daughter and no wife, I died right there on the spot—nothing left in me, nowhere to go, all used up.

Someone walked up to me and told me that the Lord would not forget me today. I honestly thought that she was an angel until I saw her again in the hospital a few days later. I called my father-in-law and tried to tell him the news but we could not finish the conversation. My Dad had been ill, and I did not want to tell him anything until I knew absolutely for sure the final outcome. So, I called B. Gray Allison.

Dr. Gray, as we affectionately called him, was the founder and president of Mid-America Baptist Theological Seminary and my boss. He had told me early on to keep my family first and had called me regularly to encourage me through these long dark days. I called and told him what I knew and he said that we needed to pray. He went through Mid-America Baptist Theological Seminary's Germantown, Tennessee campus that day and called people together for a prayer meeting in his office. There on the floor they interceded for my wife in those still moments between life and death. Back in New York, my students from the northeast campus of Mid-America came to pray for Lee Ann with me. One student, a pastor from New York City, prayed that the Lord would stop the issue of blood as He had done for the woman in the New Testament.

Hours moved slower and slower. Time stood still and I could find no comfort. My mind was spinning. Called to preach, left home and family, all for this? Three children and now my wife is gone. I drew comfort in thinking that Lee Ann would see the two children that we had lost by miscarriage. I tried to imagine what the reunion would be like as she saw in heaven the children she never saw on earth. I prayed, "O God, deliver me from death, from pain, from suffering; is there no escape?" The words of a familiar hymn returned and I was comforted once more, "Come ye sinners poor and needy, weak and wounded, sick and sore." The quiet prayers of friends calmed me as I told the Lord I wouldn't quit on Him. I am His, I will do whatever He wants. I will still praise Him even in the moment of death, defeat, or whatever comes my way.

As the evening hours began, a call came down the hall and a nurse rushed in to tell us that Lee Ann had stabilized. No more blood loss. The hospital floor was electric. Soon a doctor came to tell me that she was not out of the woods but things were much improved. I asked the doctor what happened and he looked at me and said, "Your God heard your prayers." Days later, mother and baby were home and I thought that the crisis was over. I was, however, sadly mistaken.

Although the immediate crisis had passed, the journey was not over. The doctor told me that they had taken extreme measures to preserve my wife's life and that she would be in the ICU for a long time. I was in her room several days later when she finally regained consciousness. She knew nothing of the events, long hours, prayer meetings and such. She knew that her daughter had been delivered, but nothing after that. As she awoke, unable to talk, she wrote, "What happened?" I told her in the briefest of details and she wrote "PTL" for "Praise the Lord" and she returned to sleep.

By the Gracious Working of God's Spirit

Life often seems to move from peace to crisis to recovery to peace. It does not mean that life is a crisis waiting to happen because some people live in a crisis that never ends. They just make peace with their crisis-circumstances. While people generally respond to matters in common ways, I think that some people want to correct, mend, or modify their situation. Others passively assume the role that they believe life has given them. Ironically, the prevailing culture can be a fickle judge. Is the person striving to overcome vainly jousting at windmills or are they pulling themselves up by their own bootstraps? Is the passive person living with peaceful acceptance of his situation in life, or is he taking on the persona of a permanent victim of the situation he refuses to overcome? In addition to all of this is the biblical mandate to live with the strength of the Lord according to the grace of the Lord.

How to balance strength and grace is a question that can only be answered when you run out of self. Desperation can be a great teacher, and bad news can lead to good decisions. In our personal situation I wanted the long days to end. As the caregiver I felt that I had nothing left to give. Lee Ann had the far harder course. Not being able to care for her children, especially her new daughter, compounded her frustration. And yet, our Lord always seems to give enough grace to make it through the next few minutes, hours, and even a full day. The next day the struggle began again, but the Lord's grace was always there. I remember thinking at some point that this strengthening of the Lord was like the manna given to the children of Israel in the wilderness after they left Egypt. The bread sustained them one day at a time and that was all they needed. God's grace was sustaining Lee Ann and me one day at a time and that was all we needed. Humanly speaking, I wanted the problems to end, but spiritually speaking, I found refreshment in being desperately dependent upon the Lord.

For the Transformation of the World

Lee Ann slowly recovered from her ordeal but life did not settle down for us. She came home from the hospital in time for Thanksgiving but soon was readmitted to the hospital for a severe blood clot in her leg. Our boys took it hard that Mom was going back to the hospital again. Laura was too young to understand what was happening but, needless to say, she missed her Mom. Soon Lee Ann was home from the hospital again, and it seemed that Christmas would mark the beginning of physical recovery for Lee Ann and family recovery for all of us. However, life is not always neat and convenient, or timely, or fair, or even understandable.

The day after Christmas I received a phone call from Colonel Alan Murray, my commanding officer. As an Army National Guard chaplain, I was assigned to the 3-142 CSAB (Combat Support Aviation Battalion) in Albany, New York. Colonel Murray was calling to let me know that our unit had been tasked with supporting Operation Joint Guard in Bosnia. Our unit was informed that all or part of us would be deployed to support the United Nations mission designed to end the "ethnic cleansing." The American military had already been at work there and now reserve units were being tasked to continue the mission. My immediate assignment was to counsel our soldiers as they transitioned from their full-time civilian lives to active duty. Most of us were excited about the mission, concerned about the impact on our families, and at the end of the day, anxious about the future. Family support was a critical part of the mission, so my role as chaplain would keep me busy over the next few weeks.

The final event of a long year came two days after our mobilization notice when I received a call from the Chairman of the Board of Trustees from Mid-America Baptist Theological Seminary. They related to me the stunning news that Dr. Gray Allison was retiring as our President. He was the only President I had ever known and, as the school's founder, the only President ever. The thought of his leaving was enough to rattle me, but then the chairman said that the search committee wanted to interview me. I explained that I was in the middle of a personal family crisis and that there was no way I could consider this. I was told that I was not a leading candidate but that the search committee had prayed for several months before beginning the process. They believed that the Lord wanted them to talk to several people, including, me. Would I talk with them? How could I say no to that?

Now looking back a decade after these events unfolded, it is even more apparent how loving and gracious our Lord Jesus is. My wife Lee Ann is in great health today. Though some struggles remain, she has seen the Lord triumph in her life. Our daughter is healthy but most of all she knows Jesus Christ as her personal Lord and Savior. Since 1997 I have served as President of Mid-America Seminary and the Lord has brought His dear school through many deep waters and times of celebration.

Though not usually a reflective person, I cannot help but look back on our time of extreme suffering with some measure of what it cost and what we learned. One lesson learned is the Lord is good, no matter what the outcome of circumstances. Many have lost loved ones while I had the opportunity to hold and love these dear ones long after the crisis had passed. God's grace does not mean earthly survival, because all of the redeemed will eventually be in heaven.

Another lesson brought home was the necessity of dying to self. John the Baptist knew that he had to decrease and the Lord Jesus must increase. In my opinion this lesson is one of the key aspects of Christian living, ministry, and even ministry leadership. An old cliché states that "you can get more done if no one is concerned who gets the credit." If all involved only want Jesus to be glorified and their names forgotten, amazing things can happen. I know in many difficult times, when wrestling with a decision, death to self and glory to God are guides that help one to see the light in a dark time. I would add further, that it is not only the diminishing of self but being conformed to Christ that is essential. Life looks different and people are more precious when one has a surrendered life. You can make an eternity's worth of difference in another life when you realize the value that our Creator has placed upon that life.

Finally, I will share one thought that came to me in the darkest of moments. Each year I bring my class of seminary students into my office and tell them the story of one moment of my life when life and death hung in the balance but God's grace was never in doubt. As my testimony of God's provision ends, I pray for them and leave them with the words that I remember well from the moments of blackness, "You can do more that you ever thought you could when you have to." Thank you Lord, for each day is a precious gift to walk with You until You call us home.

9

Hope That Helps
When Life Hurts

Paul Barkley

The purpose of this volume is to examine suffering and grief in a minister's life as a part of the process of spiritual formations. Following Mulholland's definition of spiritual formations as the "process of being conformed to the image of Christ by the gracious working of God's Spirit, for the transformation of the world," I will address the issue of serious health problems of one's children as a means of being conformed to the image of Christ. In facing his own struggles, the Apostle Paul said, "And now these three remain: faith, hope and love" (1 Corinthians 13:13). He also reported that the work of the Holy Spirit is to produce the fruit of love, joy, peace, patience, kindness, goodness, faithfulness, gentleness and self-control" (Galatians 5:22–23a). I want to focus on how my life experiences helped me develop hope, patience and faithfulness.

My Family and Background

My wife Rhonda and I have been married for forty-one years and have three children. Our oldest daughter, Karis, and her husband, Chad, are foreign missionaries with the International Mission Board (IMB) of the Southern Baptist Convention. Our second daughter, Kathryn, and her husband, Daryl, live near us in Cordova, Tennessee. Kathryn has her MBA degree and works in medical insurance and Daryl is an electrician. Our son, Kirk, and his wife, Dianne, live near Atlanta, where he is a drummer for a Christian artist, and she is a registered nurse. In dealing with the troubles of life, I can face my own trials much better than I can face the trials of my children, especially when I see them suffer and find that I am unable to do anything about it.

I have been a Southern Baptist pastor since 1968. I have also been involved in the field of mental health and counseling since 1971, when I went to work as a psychiatric social worker at Western State Psychiatric Hospital in Bolivar, TN. I have been a professor of religion and psychology at Baptist College of Health Sciences in Memphis, Tennessee the past fifteen years. At the same time, I maintained my private practice as Licensed Professional Counselor/Mental Health Service Provider and Licensed Marriage and Family Therapist at my counseling center, ABC (A Believer's Care) Counseling Center in Bartlett, Tennessee.

My wife and I tried to start our family for four years, going through all kinds of tests before we finally got pregnant with our first child. The pregnancy seemed to be going fine. In the fifth month of the pregnancy, I resigned my job and bi-vocational church to move to my first full-time pastorate at First Baptist Church in Adamsville, Tennessee. My wife resigned her job to stay home for the rest of the pregnancy. The baby was due on February 14. On the evening of January 5, my wife sat down on the edge of the bed at 10:30 p.m. and announced that her water just broke. Having ridden many fire department ambulances, I knew exactly what that meant. We were supposed to be going to Baptist Memorial Hospital in Memphis (two hours away on a good day) in the middle of the biggest ice storm we had had in twenty years.

We had only traveled ten miles when I saw the McNairy County General Hospital in Selmer, Tennessee. Be careful what you say. I had passed that hospital many times and remarked what a small hospital it was. I told Rhonda that I thought that we should at least stop and get her checked. When I pulled into the emergency room, the nurse told me that they did not have a doctor because of the weather. I had noticed a man standing beside a car in the doctor's parking area when we came in, so I went back out and asked him if he was a doctor. He said yes, and Dr. Harry Peeler came in to deliver our first-born child. Rhonda had already dilated to ten centimeters so they could not even prep her for the delivery. Karis was born at 12:04 a.m. on Sunday, January 6, 1974.

She was not just breach-birth; she was born rear first, weighing only two pounds, twelve ounces. The umbilical cord was wrapped around her throat three times, and the placenta was completely disintegrated. She had to stay in the hospital for a month before we could take her home. They wanted her to weigh five pounds, but let us take her home at four pounds eight ounces. A testimony to God's marvelous grace is that she never had any developmental issues and has grown-up to be a well rounded (physically, cognitively and emotionally) young lady.

Our second child, Kathryn, was born in the same hospital. We were praying for a healthy, taking-home size (over five pounds) baby. She was born five pounds, eight ounces, and we got to take home a beautiful baby daughter. At nine months, after chronic episodes of diarrhea and bronchitis, she was diagnosed with cystic fibrosis. We were told at the time that she would not live past three years and would not be able to be outside much. We were already big campers.

As a minister, it should be noted that I had already resigned First Baptist Church in Adamsville to accept the pastorate of First Baptist Church in Dyer, Tennessee. Three weeks of the month of transition were spent in the hospital with our daughter. Thanks to the miraculous grace of God, the expertise of a marvelous doctor, Dr. Aram Hanissian, and the mothering of a wonderful wife, our daughter was able to live a relatively normal life. There was the threat hanging over our heads that caused constant fear every time she would wake up in the middle of the night coughing, and you couldn't help wondering if this was the beginning of the last episode. At age thirty-one, she did eventually have to have a double lung transplant in January 2008. She got married in December of that year and is doing well today.

Our son, Kirk, is adopted, since cystic fibrosis (CF) is a disease caused by recessive genetic endowment. There would have been a twenty-five percent chance of another child having CF or a fifty-percent chance of the child at least being a carrier of the recessive gene. Kirk was your typical little boy and grew to be quite the athlete. He was into BMX bike racing, mountain biking, and played college Lacrosse at the University of Tennessee until he was knocked out three times in four months. The doctor told him that if he planned to be able to tie his shoes when he turned thirty, he should probably stop letting people hit him in the head with sticks.

This consummate athlete, at age twenty-two, got to where he could not even walk across a parking lot. When we took him to the doctor, he was diagnosed with ulcerative colitis. He did not respond to any of the conventional treatments and was even placed on a national study for a newly-developed drug. The difference in his health finally came when my wife was introduced to *The Maker's Diet*, by Dr. Jordan Rubin. My wife had gone to the only Woman's Missionary Union meeting that she could go to each year because of her work. A lady that she hardly knew gave her a book and told her she needed to read it. Thinking it was a missions book, she put it in her bag and promised to read it. It was *The Maker's Diet*. Dr.

Rubin tells his own story and my wife thought, if you would substituted Kirk's name for Dr. Rubin, it would be Kirk's story. He is on the diet now and does not take any medicine for his ulcerative colitis.

The Spiritual Journey

When Karis was born, Rhonda and I were too naïve to realize the seriousness of the situation with a two-pound-twelve-ounce baby daughter. We both simply assumed that God was going to take care of things. It did bother me at times when people would come up and tell us that "God has a purpose for this." I wanted to remind them that Job's friends did fairly well with Job when they simply came and sat in silence. It was when they opened their mouths to try to explain why God was doing what He was doing that they messed up.

Kathryn's diagnosis really rocked me to the core of my spiritual being. I will never forget the morning of July 7, 1977. I drove to the hospital in Jackson, Tennessee, to join my wife who had stayed with Kathryn, while I went home to take care of Karis. An intern had come in early that morning and blurted out that Kathryn had CF. Rhonda was by herself and called me in tears. As I rushed to the hospital, it seemed like I was going round and round with God like two ally cats with their tails tied together. I wanted to know what I had done to cause this. I told Him that if he could not get through to a hard-headed, 28-year-old Baptist preacher in any other way but to strike his innocent, nine-month-old baby girl, I wasn't interested.

In the coming couple of weeks I spent a lot of time in Job. God showed me that He introduced Job into the conversation with Satan because He knew Job's heart and character. The devil believed that if he could take trouble to Job's life, he could take Job away from God. God knew that as He brought Job through the trouble, Job would be able to see more clearly who God is and what God is able to do. The Bible says in 1 Corinthians 10:13, "No temptation [trouble or test] has seized you except what is common to man. And God is faithful; He will not let you be tempted beyond what you can bear. But when you are tempted, He will also provide a [I think better translated "the"] way out so that you can stand up under it" (NIV).

I was not unique or alone. The first chapter of James also taught me a couple of things. Verse one says, "Consider it pure joy, my brothers, whenever you face trials of many kinds" (NIV). I still struggle with the application of this but my down-home Alabama understanding is that James is saying when you have problems, throw a party. Problems are a backhanded compliment from God. They testify to His sustaining grace at work in us. For His children, God will not allow any suffering that we can't handle by His grace. The second truth came in verse 13, "When tempted, no one should say, 'God is tempting me.' For God cannot be tempted by evil, nor does he tempt anyone" (NIV). My omnipotent God does not need to tempt or test me to figure out what I am going to do. He simply sometimes allows Satan to sift us so that we will be able to see the mighty hand of God at work.

God communicated this to me in the most unusual way. I had gone home to Adamsville from the hospital in Memphis, where Kathryn was by this time. Remember, we were in the month of transition to a new church field. I had a pretty big garden and the corn needed picking. I had picked it and was sitting on the front porch shucking it. I noticed that every time I got a dried-up ear of corn, it did not have any worms. But every time I came to a juicy, filled-out ear, it had worms. God could not have spoken any clearer if the sky had opened up the sky and a big booming voice had said: "Son, this is what I have been trying to show you. The devil, like the worms, is not interested in the dried-up ears; he wants the juicy, filled out ears. Kathryn has all the grace and strength that she needs to deal with this or I would not have allowed her to have it." That day I began to share with people that I believed that she would not be cured of the CF, but that she would be able to live as though she does not have it. Kathryn heard this so often that she began to tell people that she believed that she was going to live to be eighty and get run over by a bus crossing the street.

I do not mean to imply that it has become easy and that I do not worry. I must always look to God for strength. Even Jesus in the garden, as He faced the impending suffering of the cross, was "exceeding sorrowful, even to death" (Matthew 26:38, KJV). In agony "His sweat was as it were great drops of blood falling to the ground" (KJV). He asked His Father, if it were possible, to take the suffering away. Yet Jesus wanted to do the Father's will. The writer of Hebrews reminds us that Jesus "for the joy set before him *endured* the cross, scorning the shame" (Hebrews 12:2, NIV). My hope had come from the concept that the Great God of the universe—the sovereign God of creation, my Heavenly Father—knows me better than I know myself, loves me more than I love myself, and desires my best good more than I desire it. His will for me is what is best for me. John Greenleaf Whittier, the beloved New England poet wrote in *The Eternal Goodness*:

Yet, in the maddening maze of things,
And tossed by storm and flood,
To one fixed trust my Spirit clings,
I know that God is Good.

The Concern of Being Consumed in the Crucible of Life

The daily lives of many of us is a cockney of confusing and consuming crises. If you have not arrived at this place in life, hang on. It is coming! The struggle for many of us is to stand in the onslaught. It is tempting to cringe in fear, retreat in defeat and wallow in our woundedness. We begin to feel as thought no one else in all of the history of the world has had the problems that continue to confront us. I encounter families every week who have become stranded in the struggle. They cannot see any way out of the problem.

I have four things that I want to attempt to communicate. First of all, we are not unspiritual or uneducated simply because we are confused. The Book of Job addressed the question that many of us have asked: "What did I do to deserve this?" We all want an answer to the "Why?" question. I do not believe that God is offended by our honest and genuine questions. I am a little put off by people who seem to have simplistic and sloppy spiritual answers. I am much more comforted by those who simply come alongside me and say that they care. Those who attempt to give "God's" explanation for Him bother me. "God has a plan in all this" even when spoken in sincerity can sound shallow and hollow in the face of my real pain. Those who come and sit in silence, like Job's three friends did for the first week, often bring the most comfort and strength.

During times of trouble there may be some who come to us with the unsatisfactory suggestion of stoical submission. This is the second truth I have discovered in suffering. While I acknowledge that God's ways are higher than my ways and His thoughts are higher than my thoughts, this strategy seems to imply to me that I am somehow responsible for this crisis. I must say here that I am thinking of things like Hurricane Katrina or the terminal illness of a child. In the crucible of these types of situations, stoical submission seems to deny the tender relationship that I have developed with a loving heavenly Father.

The third truth that I have found in the struggle comes through those whom I have identified as the purveyors of pious platitudes. The well-meaning friends will go to a verse like Romans 8:28, "All things work together for good." They admonish me to know that true spirituality would see the silver lining that God is working out some grand plan in the midst of my calamity. I know that the writer of Hebrews said that it was the joy that waited on the other side that gave Jesus the strength to endure the cross. In my spiritual weakness I need the "other comforter" to come alongside me, wrap me in His righteous arms, and assure me that this also will pass. This does not minimize my pain, but it does comfort me and give me hope.

The fourth and final truth that I have found in the crucible of life is that my loving Father desires my best good more that I want it myself. Miss Bertha Smith, the Southern Baptist missionary who witnessed the great Shantung Revival in China and came back to America to tell of it, taught me a truth a long time ago. I heard her say that we should never pray for God to bless us as though we had to overcome His reluctance. She said that we should pray simply that we become "blessable." God in His omniscience knows what my best good is more that I do. In His omnipotence He is more able to produce it than I am. In the words of an old gospel song:

My God is too good to be unkind.
My God is too smart to make a mistake.
Therefore, when I cannot trace the hand of God,
I can always trust the Heart of God.

Confusion in Crisis and Questions Unanswered

I will celebrate forty years in the ministry as a Baptist preacher this year. I pastored churches in West Tennessee for twenty-five years. I have been a counselor and therapist for the past thirty-five years. I have been teaching psychology and religion at a Baptist college for the past fifteen years. I remind the reader of this so that you can put some of my struggles into perspective.

Most of us are knocked off balance by the really hard blows that can be inflicted upon us by life. My wife and I have been confronted by many challenges through the health of our children. Our first daughter was born seven weeks premature in a small hospital eighty miles from the major hospital where she was supposed to be delivered by a doctor that we had never met until that very moment. Our second child was diagnosed with cystic fibrosis when she was nine months old, and we were told that she would not live to be three (she is thirty-two today and had a very successful double lung transplant a little over a year ago). Our third child, an adopted son, was diagnosed a few years ago with ulcerative colitis, and we almost lost him.

I do not share these things with you again to garner your sympathy, but rather to put three personal observations in perspective from my life experience. I also hope that some who have experienced the losses due to the storms and struggles can identify and find some degree of encouragement.

The first is a question. Is it wrong to doubt your beliefs or your faith? When life seems to crash in around us and there seems to be little hope on the horizon, many will reflect on the words of some preacher that said if we would trust God, He would take care of us. When God seems to be a million miles away from your life circumstances, what do you do? Someone once said, "It is not wrong to doubt your beliefs, but problems come when you believe your doubts." Doubting your beliefs is tantamount to testing your faith. God invites us to try Him and test Him. Our God is a big God and can stand up to any honest scrutiny. Even Jesus on the cross cried out, "My God, My God, why have you forsaken me?"

The inability to find a satisfactory answer to the question leads to my second observation of people in crisis. Crises are usually accompanied by a sense of impending, overwhelming destruction, defeat and discouragement. There is not really anything wrong with this feeling. There would probably be something seriously wrong with a person who did not feel these emotions in the midst of the crucible of crisis.

The third observation comes from a question that Jesus asked the disciples, "Will you also leave me?" The disciples' answer was very telling: "Lord, where would we go? You alone have the answers to life's greatest questions." In the center of our doubt, we must walk entirely by faith. Even though I cannot make sense of it, even though I cannot see the real possibility of any hope at the end of my rope, I find the one who is my rock of ages and my firm foundation. The world does not understand, but the believer has a strength that holds in the storm in spite of the doubts, fears, defeats and discouragement of the present situation.

Mrs. Joyce Rogers was interviewed by our pastor in one of our recent worship services. She was talking about her new book to help widows deal with their grief. She related one of the main things that she remembered her late husband, Dr. Adrian Rogers said often: "You can't understand that Jesus is all that you need until He is all that you have." In this context I would put it another way. You cannot *find* your hope until your *face* your hopelessness.

"But It's Not Fair!"

I do not know how many times I have heard this phrase in my counseling office or when I have made a pastoral visit. When something bad occurs in our life and we have difficulty understanding, we are all tempted to complain, "It's not fair!" As Christians face calamity and sorrow, we often ask God what we did to deserve this problem. We are God's people, yet so many in the world who care nothing for God don't seem to face near as many problems as we have!

As I have served people in my forty years of ministry, many have asked the question seemingly implied by the Book of Job. "Why do bad things happen to good people?" The implication is that there is some kind of cosmic bookkeeping system that balances out the good and bad in people's lives based on personal behavior. I am not sure where this idea started, but it has a long history. I remember seeing a papyrus of the "judgment" that my wife and I picked up in Egypt a few years ago. It depicts the departed body on a table as the priest removes the heart for the embalming process. There is a set of balances near by with a feather on one scale. The heart is to be placed on the other scale. The crocodile is waiting, and if the heart is not lighter than the feather, the crocodile eats the heart and the departed cannot enter the after life.

This human mindset seems to be programmed into the DNA of all humans. It gives us the distorted perspective that when you are good, God will bless you. But when you are bad, God will get you. This seems to logically come from what some have called the "law of the harvest." "A man reaps what he sows" (Galatians 6:7, NIV). While I do very much believe in individual accountability, I do not believe that every bad thing that happens in life is the direct result of my bad choice or behavior.

We live in a fallen world, among fallen people, and we are all fallen human beings. Some of the bad things that happen come from the bad choices of other fallen creatures. Take the drunk driver who hits and kills an innocent child. Some of the bad things come from a fallen universe that is still reeling from the effects of the Fall. I think some of the climate problems, flooding, and forest fires that we experience might fall in this category. I also think that we sometimes miss the fact that the evil that befalls Job is brought at the hand of the Evil One himself who is still alive and well on planet Earth.

As we all struggle to make sense of our individual dilemmas, we need to realize that life is *not fair*. Never has been! Never will be! And to be honest, we would not want it to be. As fallen human beings, our sin deserves death and separation from God. We do not want what we deserve—what is *fair*. We want grace and mercy. Life will continue to confound us. There will probably never be a satisfactory answer to the "Why?" question. But we can rest in God and trust Him to always to do what is right and good. To accept this fact will place us in a position for God to be able to minister His mercy and grace to us by that peace that passes all understanding.

Joy, Hope, and Faithfulness

The latest developments with our children have proved to carry out the continuation of the process that God has seemed to want for us. Karis and her husband had tried for four or five years to start their family. Finally, last year, the result of the third in vitro fertilization, they presented us with our first grandchild. She was a perfectly beautiful, healthy baby girl that they named Eliana Rhys (from the Hebrew *eliana* for "God answered our prayers" and from the Gaelic for *active*, which she was in the womb).

Kathryn did get married on December 27, 2008. When she got her lungs, we knew that the lungs had CMV (Cyto Megala Virus) and Kathryn did not. Kathryn had to be given CMV so that she would not reject the lungs. Everything seemed to be going fine until the week of Thanksgiving, when she developed severe abdominal cramping and nausea. The transplant team first told her it was just anxiety about the wedding and they started her on some anti-anxiety meds. She did not get any better and went to the doctor the Monday before Christmas. The doctors did an ultrasound and told her that her gallbladder had to be removed. She was hoping that it could be done after the wedding and honeymoon. They said "No; now! We are booking a room for you right now." By 7:00 p.m. she no longer had a gallbladder. The pain and nausea did not subside. The day of her wedding we got her down the aisle on nausea and pain meds. She went straight from the reception to the hospital where she stayed for six weeks. As of June 2009, the doctors believe that they finally have a handle on the situation; she is free of pain this week and beginning to gain some weight.

Kirk had another episode back in January, when his white blood count, red blood count, and platelets all bottomed out. He was hospitalized to run tests. The bone marrow biopsy was negative for leukemia—and were we grateful. The doctors had no explanation for his blood levels. He was put on high doses of prednisone and the blood levels eventually began to come back up. However, when he was taken off the prednisone too fast the numbers went back down. Both his hematologist and rheumatologist say he is an anomaly. He is back on moderate doses of prednisone with the hopes of gradually taking it away. Since he plays for a Christian musician and will be away from home for long stints this summer, we are concerned about his continued recovery.

In the face of the continuing complications of our children's health issues, where does one find hope, patience and faith? I learned two truths years ago from Luke's account of Jesus stilling the storm in Luke 8:22–25. In the first place, Jesus said in verse 22, "Let's go over to the other side of the lake" (NIV). In the storms of our lives it is easy to overlook His promise. He said He would never leave us. Christ will stay with us to the end. If the disciples had remembered in the middle of the storm that Jesus had said they were going to the other side, they might not have been as afraid.

The second truth I heard Henry Blackaby teach on several occasions. Peace is a person. It is not a proposition, or a truth, or a doctrine. Blackaby said frequently, in the storms of life, we need to remember that Peace is asleep in the back of the boat. The important foundation for my hope is my relationship with the One who still the storms. The testing of our faith that is talked about in the first chapter of James is not to see if we will fail, but rather to determine if our trust will take us through the trouble. It is not my great faith that sees me through, but my faithful God. He is great and good and does all things well. I must anchor my hope in Him.

I can honestly say that I have had joy in my journey even when I have not always been happy. Some will ask how one can have joy when he is not happy. I would in turn ask, "Did Jesus always have joy?" I would propose that the answer is "yes." Did Jesus have joy in Gethsemane? Again, my answer would be "yes." Happiness is like a thermometer; it only registers the circumstances around it. Joy is more like a thermostat; it changes the attitude around the circumstances. Joy comes from the calm assurance that my loving heavenly Father always has me in the grip of his protection. We find ourselves in the position of the three Hebrew children in Daniel 3:16–18:

> O Nebuchadnezzar, we do not need to defend ourselves before you in this matter. If we are thrown into the blazing furnace, the God we serve is able to save us from it, and he will rescue us from your hand, O King. But even if he does not, we want you to know, O king, that we will not serve your gods or worship the image of gold you have set up (NIV).

My hope comes from the loving relationship that I have with my heavenly Father who loved me so much that he came chasing after me before I ever came looking for Him. He chased me not to hurt or harm me, but always to redeem and help me. The world and my circumstances did not give that hope to me and they cannot take it from me.

Part Two

Physicians' Contributions

10

Facing the Realities
Of Suffering and Death

Scott Morris

All life is suffering. The Book of Job states that human life is short and full of "trouble as the sparks fly upward" (Job 5:7, KJV). I am a physician and there are days when I treat one patient after another with a terrible problem for which there is no clear relief. On these days it seems as though relentless suffering is the fate of us all. I am, however, also an ordained United Methodist minister, and I believe deep down that the core of human existence is not suffering but joy. God has created us for joy. Not a giddy joy that children experience at the fair, but a type of joy that grows from the experience of knowing and loving God, and the experience of the goodness and the love of God for His own. We are made for joy, but in this fallen world we are met with much suffering. Bouncing between these two poles is how I live my daily life and how spiritual formation has shaped my life.

Life's Experiences

I was a senior in high school when my mother was diagnosed with ovarian cancer. At the time she was told she would have ten years to live. About six months later she became extremely ill and was told she would live only one year. Six months later she died. As an only child, I had spent many hours alone, or so I thought. In reality, my mother was always present in some fashion. She looked out for me in every way she could, yet when she got sick, I felt I had no way to help her. As a teenager, I did not fully understand her illness and regret to this day that I was not at her bed when she died. It is not as though I believe I could have changed the outcome, but I have always felt I somehow let her down. This is a form of grief that many people experience and often do not fully resolve.

For all of us, how we assimilate the experience of our parents' death or the death of someone else we love, shapes the way we view and experience life. In America, our culture has come to see death as the ultimate enemy to be avoided at all cost. Death is not to be talked about by families, not to be discussed in church, not to be allowed by physicians, not to be blessed by clergy until all hope is lost. This is not a healthy state.

Physicians have promised that new technology will prolong life indefinitely, and when someone we love is near death, our first response is "do whatever can be done to save the life we love." Unfortunately, our new technology can often prolong life functions but not necessarily the quality of life needed to fully experience love.

Juan Marcos is a patient of mine who immigrated to America from the Philippines fifteen years ago. He is now 75 years old and works for minimum wage at McDonalds. While walking to work, he was hit by a car and fell into a coma. He was placed on a ventilator and given life support until his family could arrive from the Philippines to see him one last time. Once here, they refused to turn the machines off and he stayed on the breathing machine for two months. Finally, he slowly got better and was able to breath on his own. His family considered it a miracle. He improved enough to leave the hospital and now lives with his daughter. The rest of the family has returned home. When he comes to see me in our clinic, he is now in a wheelchair, he breathes through a tracheostomy, his head is slumped over, and he looks at me with questioning eyes and asks "why did you let them do this to me?" What am I to say? I know that the right thing was to let him die and go to God, but we are not spiritually strong enough to believe that God's all-embracing arms are waiting.

Juan's experience, thankfully, is not the only way. Several years ago one of my physician partners, Febe Wallace, went with her husband and three-year-old son, Scott, on a skiing vacation to Colorado. While there, Scott became sick and Febe took him to the pediatrician. The pediatrician was not quite sure what to make of Scott's illness, so Febe asked him to draw blood so she could look at it herself. Under the microscope she saw what she feared the most. Scott had leukemia.

The family flew back home to Memphis and Scott was admitted to St. Jude's Children's Research Hospital. Scott immediately began treatment and was doing well until the fifth day of the treatment. On a Saturday morning, Febe was holding Scott in her arms and his body went limp. She knew what had happened. As a side effect of the treatment a blood vessel broke in his brain and he had a large stroke. Febe called me and asked me to come to the hospital. I remember that day well. It was my 41st birthday.

As I walked into the intensive care unit, I could see Scott's CT scan from across the room. Even if he were to recover from the leukemia, the stroke would leave him with terrible problems. We had to make a decision. If she kept him on the ventilator, his brain would stabilize and he would keep breathing. Febe and Tom (her husband) had to decide what to do. There was no hesitation. We gathered around Scott's bed and the doctor turned off the machine. Febe then held him in her arms as he took his last breath. It was then my job to conduct the funeral. What do you say about a three year old boy? He knew his colors, he loved his mommy. I have often thought about that day and the strength of character I saw in Febe. I have no doubt whatsoever she did the right thing. She gave up what she loved most in the world into the care of the One whom she believes loved her in a way beyond understanding. It is from such grief that I have, over time, come to better understand God's love for me and our broken world.

William Sloane Coffin, Jr. preached a famous sermon at Riverside Church in New York City the Sunday after his youngest son died in a tragic car crash in Boston. At the funeral, a woman came up to comfort Rev. Coffin, patted his back, and claimed that the death must have been God's will. In his sermon, Coffin was comforted only by the knowledge that since God himself has known the death of a Son, as Coffin's son died, it was God's heart that was the first to break. Such grief is never easy. It should never be trivialized by platitudes. But, grief can be a window to God's heart. He understands pain and sorrow. He gave up His own Son to die on the cross. Grief and suffering can point us to the true nature of God's passion which heals and comforts all who come to Him who are wounded and broken. God so loved the world that He gave us His Son. And it is because of the suffering of Christ that we can know the joy of everlasting life.

As a medical student and physician-in-training, I was not taught to see the link between compassion and suffering in a way that leads to healing. I was told that as a physician I was expected to keep an objective distance in order to avoid letting my emotions cloud my judgment.

As a third year medical student, I was on rounds with a learned professor and group of residents and students. When it came time to discuss the status of patient Vera Jones, one of my fellow medical students, Sarah Whitney, stepped forward to review her case. Sarah not only told of the results of Ms. Jones blood tests and CT scan, but also spoke of her family and her fears. Before she could finish, the attending physician cut her off and said, "Dr. Whitney, I am afraid you have lost your objectivity. You have let yourself get too close to this patient." No one said a word, and Sarah bowed her head and took her place in the back of the pack.

At the time, I knew what was said was wrong and today I know it is intrinsically wrong. No one needs to be taught how to keep their distance from another human being. That comes naturally. Our objectivity is never clouded by better understanding what brings joy and life to a person whose health care is in our hands. What we need to be taught is how to get close to another human being! That is something few of us do well, and it is something that even fewer physicians do very well. The attending physician that day may have been a skilled medical diagnostician, but he failed at teaching a young doctor the art of caring for the health of another.

Life's Lessons

My own lessons in caring have often come from patients who consider me to be their doctor. This has been especially true over the last twenty years as I have been the physician for many older, hard-working African Americans, who grew up in a segregated South. For many, I am the first doctor they could call their own. Often, the women have raised two families—their own children and the children of the family for whom they worked as housekeeper. On too many occasions, they have left their own children at home when the children were sick in order to tend to the sick children of their employers. Suffering and grief are a part of their everyday life. Because of discrimination and poverty, the luxury of taking the time to grieve over death or other important losses has not been an option. Nevertheless, and remarkably in my mind, these strong souls have not chosen a path that leads to bitterness. Instead, if I ask "How are you doing?" the answer I most often hear is: "I am *fine* and *blessed*!" Fine and blessed when there is no money, no other resources, even when children are estranged and the rent is due. As one of my former colleagues described it, what there is in abundance is spiritual "capital."

This spiritual capital, I believe, comes from depending solely on God's love in Christ as a source of comfort. This is a form of spiritual direction that can only come from daily dependence on the non-material world— walking by faith in the light of the gospel. Because I am now accustomed to caring for people who are "fine and blessed," I spend half of my appointed time with them making sure I have done what is needed to care for their physical problems. The rest of the time is employed either helping them spend some of this "spiritual capital" on their physical health or trying to learn how I, too, may become fine and blessed.

One of the first such patients who became a patient-teacher was Robert Thomas, one of the first people I diagnosed with AIDS. This was before the current round of effective AIDS drugs that make AIDS a manageable disease. When Robert was diagnosed, it was an almost certain death sentence. When I told Robert his diagnosis, he was working as a yard man for a wealthy family. He received the news in a very matter-of-fact way. There were no tears and no sense of despondency which is often the case even today. Over time, Robert kept all of his appointments and was always cheerful whenever I saw him. He was so upbeat that I began to worry that he did not fully understand his diagnosis. So, one day I sat on my stool and touched his hand. I looked him in the eye and said, "Do you understand your problem?" He looked back with comfort in his eyes for me and said, "I understand my problem and I know that God loves me." The depth of Robert's faith and certainty about God's love is something I have seen many times from other patients who have little of material value that the world would hold dear. But, these have reached a level of spiritual wholeness that I envy and that even comforts me.

I am afraid that the process of becoming a physician affected me in ways that are difficult to undo. While I entered medical school fully intent on not letting the intellectualization of creation affect me, I found myself, like most other students, being gradually persuaded by the *religion of medicine*. The realization of how far I had been converted came to me on a day I was called to do CPR on an elderly woman at Grady Memorial Hospital in Atlanta. I was the first to arrive in her room and began doing chest compressions while the rest of the Harvey Team came rushing in. Together, everyone assumed their task and the mechanistic process of resussitation unfolded. Then one of the residents began talking about going to get pizza when we were done. I found myself thinking about what kind of pizza I wanted and placed my order along with the others. Despite our best efforts, the woman died and still, afterwards, I went with the others to share a pizza. It was only later that I felt sick that the life of another human being was slipping away under my hands while I was trivially thinking about dinner and wanting to fit in with the other students. Thankfully, I realized what had happened almost instantly, but the lure of forgetting about the sacredness of life is ever present.

Conclusion

Over the last few years, I have had my own medical problems to cope with and I have found that the presence of chronic pain can be a challenge to one's spiritual strength. In the last seven years, I have gone from doing daily exercise and playing sports to having both my hip and my knee replaced. The challenges of my surgeries and the onset of arthritis leave me with chronic pain that is at times extremely distracting. It is not so easy to think only of God or focus on prayer when pain is present without relief. Yet, it is only through my winding path of spiritual formation that I can keep my focus on the things that matter.

My wife's constant encouragement, my friends' and colleagues' commitment to ministry and my daily experience of caring for the poor makes life full in the way I suspect God intended. The constant pain prevents me from ever feeling totally carefree. In fact, it is a useful way of showing my patients that I actually do understand what they are experiencing, at least in part. Throughout the day, I often show off the scar on my right knee and talk of my problems with people who feel no one understands. Still I am left with both the tragedy and blessedness of life in ways that show my spiritual formation is still developing as a follower of Christ Jesus.

Recently, a young Mexican mother brought her two young children to our clinic. The mother spoke no English so her 8-year-old daughter, Chastity, was my translator. Chastity's 18-month-old sister had a cold. I calmly told the mother through Chastity that the cold would soon be gone and that antibiotics would not make her better and neither would over the counter cold medicines. I gave her some simple ways to manage and reassured her about the baby. Chastity then told me that she had been having a stomach ache. I asked a few more questions and suddenly realized that Chastity, her sister and her mother were living in a homeless shelter. I looked at Chastity and asked, "Why are you living there, what happened to your home?" And then, out of the mouth of an 8-year-old came the saddest words I have ever heard. Chastity came close to me and looked at me with her brown eyes and said, "Our daddy found someone else, and he don't love us no more."

I fell silent for I did not know what to say or do. I just reached out and held her hand and patted her mother's leg. Next, I made a phone call to the pastor of a newly formed Hispanic church. I told him Chastity's story and he said he would send someone immediately to get the family. I could not make Chastity's father love her again, but before the sun set, she was out of the homeless shelter and in the arms of a community of faith that would point her to Christ and teach her new ways of loving.

This has in many ways been my own experience of God's love and the joy of life. Grief and suffering is something I experience in some ways almost every day. My own personal trials have at times been difficult, but then life again draws joy back into my world.

After 25 years as a physician, I am comfortable in making decisions that affect people in profound ways. I am good at delivering bad news, but

I know without question that living with grief and suffering requires the strength of a community of friends and lovers in order to keep joy alive. My own spiritual formation has been a rocky road that has kept me looking to God, which is how I believe He intended it to be.

I I

A Country Doctor's Perspective On Grief and Suffering

Wayne Rhear

From time to time I have been asked to write something about various subjects that pertain to my God-called profession—the practice of medicine. At particular times I have mixed emotions about how to respond to the request, depending on the nature of the subject matter. On this occasion I have been asked to share my opinions, feelings and insights regarding the subject of suffering. As a practicing Family Practice Physician for over thirty-five years, God has placed me in a front row seat (so to speak) where I have witnessed just about every form of suffering. These various issues affect the lives of the precious patients that God has sent through the front doors of my office. I believe and must emphasize that when I refer to my office, it is truly not my office but God's office. He called me into the practice of medicine to minister to those that are sick in mind, body and soul. I am just an instrument that He has designed to carry out His ministry to those that need help. God runs my practice and I pray I never lose sight of who He is and most importantly who I am—just an instrument for His use.

In a medical practice, a team effort must exist. I would be remiss if I did not tell you about my earthly partner in practice—my wife, Judy. She has been there for me during the good times and through some very dark times where suffering seemed to be the order of the day. However, with

God's direction and her help, we made it through the tough times. At this stage of my life, I am now involved in what might possibly be the most challenging and exciting work that God has ever called me to do.

First of all, I still have my regular practice. I have working with me two fine Christian Advanced Nurse Practitioners (APNs) and a compassionate Christian support staff. To see them use their hands, which are really God's, and to minister to those in need, is very fulfilling to me.

Second, and possibly closest to my heart, is my role as Medical Director for three long-term care facilities (nursing homes). With this comes the responsibility for about 200 of the most wonderful, loving, patients anyone could ever desire.

For many of these patients, suffering is a way of life every day until God reaches down with his loving and tender hands to take them home. It never ceases to amaze me, however, at the strength, tenacity of life, and spiritual depth these patients possess. Where does all of this inner strength originate? Is it genetic? Is it a reflection of "their raising" (as we say in the South)? Does it come from their deep spiritual roots that were instilled in them by God-fearing parents? Parents who dared to "draw the line" between right and wrong and not apologize for knowing and following a wonderful Savior, Jesus Christ? I think it is probably a combination of all of these things. They have a depth of wisdom that many times goes unnoticed because of the tendency in our society to say, "Well, they are just old people without much to offer."

You might ask me if I suffer. The answer is yes. Yes I suffer when I see any member of my family suffering. Their suffering is my suffering. I suffer when I see a dying patient whose body in worn out from years of hard work and the stresses of life. I ask myself, "*Can* I do more to relieve their suffering?" "*Could* I have done more to relieve their suffering before their final journey to God's side?" I suffer when I see friends who are in financial, physical and spiritual battles. I want to offer sympathy to them but I know their suffering is a matter God will handle. If I can understand that truth, then I can understand that my job is to be there for them in the midst of their suffering while God cares for them and heals their suffering.

I pray that comments made in the following pages will guide you along your way as you seek to help those around you who suffer. I hope that you too will answer God's call and forever seek His perfect will for your life. My plan is to present you a thought process that will hopefully help you find "evidence based answers" concerning the way to deal with suffering in your own life and in the lives of those whom God has assigned to your care.

Definition of Suffering

Allow me to return to the comments noted in the introduction. These concern an "evidence based" thought process used to evaluate and understand suffering. First of all, one must have a definition of suffering, and I go back to my old *Webster's Collegiate Dictionary* (1953) for a clear explanation of the meaning of the word. *Suffering* is: "(1) to undergo pain of body or mind, (2) to endure or tolerate an evil or injury, (3) to sustain loss." Generally, our thoughts may gravitate to the first definition. Most assuredly in medicine, one sees suffering in the form of pain in the human body possibly from injuries received in a severe automobile accident. Patients with severe infections or terminal diseases can certainly exhibit suffering in the form of pain. One cannot forget those patients who suffer from altered minds secondary to accidental injury, intentional injury due to drugs, or carnal abuse of the body secondary to sexually transmitted diseases. Another sad set of circumstances present themselves when you deal with suffering in a patient who is totally innocent of any wrong doing. And their suffering has been inflicted on them by physical abuse by irresponsible parents who deal in drugs or sexual misconduct. Certainly, definition three has a definite place in any considerations of suffering because we have all seen these devastating effects on people when they suffer the loss of a loved one.

Etiology of Suffering

It is time for another definition. *Etiology* means the assignment of a reason or cause for an illness. In medicine, when the physician looks for clues that lead to proper treatment of various illnesses, he or she must deal with a process to consider reasons and/or causes of the suffering created by the disease process. It is very important to identify the etiology of the suffering that we are considering. The burning question that must be the focus in our search for answers is *why* do people suffer? About twenty-five years ago I heard a sermon on suffering and its causes by Charles Stanley—noted pastor, teacher, and preacher. He asked the question: "Why do people suffer?" His answers have been a clear guide for me as I deal with suffering in my patients as well as my own life.

His answers were precise and clear. There are four main reasons why people suffer, and, I remember them as follows. First, people suffer because of parental disobedience to God's laws. I have seen this all too often in the emergency room. It is evident in the school systems where the use of drugs by irresponsible parents during pregnancy—such as crack, cocaine, or alcohol—severely affect the life of a newborn. These were manifest in the form of devastating physical and psychological defects in that newborn child. Physical problems such as low birth weight, prematurity, micro-cephaly (small brain), and sexually transmitted diseases are passed to the newly born child. All of these are difficult issues indeed.

Probably some of the saddest issues are the psychological defects that begin to show up in the early school years, such as decreased ability to concentrate, agitated states of mind, and an inability to communicate with teachers or peers. These children are virtually impossible to teach and usually end up in special education classes or alternative schools. Sometimes, and even more tragically, they drop out of school when they are of age. All of this suffering stems from irresponsible behavior of the parents. They turn their back on God and to the responsibilities He has given them—the children to be reared in a loving Christian home.

The second reason people suffer is because of God's chastisement for rebellious behavior against His laws and will. This can be seen in the Old Testament when studying the activities of Israel—*the apple of God's eye.* Israel would go through a period of loving and obeying God. But over the course of time, the nation would forget how richly God had blessed them. Then they began to feel that *they could make it on their own without God,* and their focus turned away from God and His provisions. Then they held to their selfish inward thoughts, their open rebellion against God, their apathy to God's direction, and eventually, God's chastisement would fall with its own innate and unique sufferings. Pagan practices would creep into Israel's fabric and put the nation into bondage to Satan. God chastised them time and again for allowing pagan ideas and practices to come into the nation and destroy it. This brought about great suffering to the nation of Israel.

Third, suffering can be caused by direct disobedience of God's physical laws. God created humankind with a healthy body and mind. However, satanic forces can destroy what God has created. People do not understand and follow God's directions for their life. They fail to protect the holy temple, their physical body, which God has given them. I have seen this many, many times in patients who have abused their bodies with drugs, alcohol, or tobacco. I have been at the bedside of a patient with end-stage lung disease caused by smoking tobacco for years. Their suffering was horrible to watch. They had destroyed God's design of healthy lung tissue and eventually lost their life because of disobedience. I have watched non-compliant diabetics die of the severe complication of uncontrolled diabetes. This happened because they did not take proper care of God's holy temple—their body.

Fourth is simply suffering that is allowed or created only for the glory of God. The prime example of this kind of suffering is illustrated in the life of Job. Job was a righteous and upstanding man of God. But Satan was allowed to attack him by taking away his family, his wealth and his health. If you try to find a reason for Job's suffering, it would be different, especially if you were looking for a "worldly" reason. Only when you can understand that Job—in the end—was faithful to God does it make any sense. And Satan lost the battle to take Job's loyalty away from his heavenly Father. Job's suffering was for the glory of God.

I have treated many faithful and loyal servants of Christ for disease processes that came through no fault of their own. Diseases such as cancer or premature heart disease or lung disease were among those maladies that these patients faced. They suffered from the side effects of these debilitating illnesses. I have been inspired by the courage of these patients. Their trust was in God. They blamed no one but kept their focus on their heavenly Father for the strength they needed to get through each day.

Approach to Dealing with Suffering

After dealing with the evaluation and search for a possible etiology of suffering, the state of suffering itself must be measured against the causes and/or reasons of suffering the person is enduring. During our medical school training, we were drilled and challenged constantly, day and night for three and a half years, in symptoms and signs of every possible disease. Night after night, page after page, we searched through medical textbooks and patient's charts for causes and reasons for a patient's disease processes which could produce a state of suffering in our patient. After about three years into our training, I felt that I had been thoroughly taught and prepared to take care of patients. These three major aspects of the patient were the *physical, sociological* and *psychological.*

Physical

First, we had to look at the *physical* man when we began our evaluation. Having been through gross anatomy, biochemistry, pathology, endocrinology, radiology, obstetrics and gynecology, pediatrics, cardiology, and surgery, we had a fairly good grasp of what signs and symptoms we were to consider in the very ill. Time and experience would help us to a more thorough understanding of the physical aspects of their illness. Interestingly, after thirty-five years of practice I am still learning new things about the human body every day.

Sociological

Secondly, a good physician had to understand the *sociological* man. Who were his parents? Where was he born? Where did he live? Was he married? Did he have children? Did he have a job that would support the family? Was he homeless without the privilege of having access to any of the above benefits? Information about this aspect of your patient is vitally important in predicting how the patient would be able to respond to your plan of therapy. You might be up against problems such as: no job, therefore no money to buy the medication you prescribe; no car, therefore no way to keep scheduled recheck appointments; no family, therefore no support system. No one to love them equals no one to care for them. You can enter into the patient's suffering in these situations.

Psycological

Thirdly, one must understand the *psychological* man. The physician must look at the pressures the patient faces every day. What you are dealing with is this: psychologically, how will this patient deal with the physical as well as the sociological aspects of their care. Is he angry about the situation? Is he in denial and totally convinced that perhaps there is nothing wrong? Is he in despair over his situation? Is he depressed?

I heard an excellent definition of depression from a well-known and respected pastor of our time, Adrian Rogers, deceased pastor of Bellevue Baptist Church, Memphis, Tennessee. He mentioned it in one of his sermons. It was a short and simple description of the progression of circumstances that lead one into the pit of depression. First there is a feeling of *helplessness*. There seems to be no way out of the person's helplessness. Then there is *hopelessness*. There seems to be no one to whom the person can turn for help. Then there is the final feeling of *sadness*. If anyone has ever experienced depression, the depth of the depression is certainly understandable. One can understand how on a bright sunny day, everything around you can seem dark and empty.

The Missing Piece

After three years of looking at the patient from the three aspects noted above, I began to believe that something was missing. There was something that modern medical training was not addressing. I finally found that missing piece in one of those Saturday lectures that I almost skipped. I was in training at University of Tennessee, College of Health Sciences, Memphis, Tennessee. I had been up all night delivering babies, and my

physical strength was fading quickly. However, since it was a required class
I felt that I had to attend. So, I found a seat in the back of the lecture
room in the darkest corner and prepared myself to get a good hour's sleep.
I thought it would be the most boring psychiatric lecture known to man.
But there was something different about this psychiatrist. He talked about
the *physical, sociological* and *psychological* aspects of humanity. I said to myself: "Here we go again!" But he caught my attention when he stated that
there is one more aspect of man that you have not yet considered. This
aspect is the glue that binds the other threes together. By then I was fully
awake and had my pencil out ready to record something that I had not
heard in my three years of training. He said; "Unless you understand the
spiritual aspect of man you will never be able to successfully treat any patient you will see in the future."

There it was! *Spiritual* man is the key to understanding and treating the total patient. Where is his heart, where is his mind, where is his
will? Who controls his spiritual life? Is it Satan or is it God? Where his
heart, mind, and will are, will be the determining factors in how your patient will respond to your treatment. This is especially important when you
are treating a patient suffering from a physical or a spiritual problem. The
physician can prescribe medication and a course of therapy, but his efforts
are all in vain if the patient's mind and will are determined to *do their own
thing.* If a patient has heart, mind, or will problems, trying to control his
suffering is futile. A patient who has a strong spiritual conviction of heart
and mind and will focused on God will be a patient able to bear suffering
well and conquer it.

Assessment of Suffering

Let us think for a time about assessing that patient, student, or church
member that comes to your office seeking help in a time of great need and
suffering in their life. They might say, "what can I do? I feel helpless, I can't
see a way out of this time of suffering, I feel hopeless and all of this has
made me sad and depressed." You feel this hurt! You can feel this suffering!
What is our part in helping these suffering people?

In the medical assessment of the suffering patient it is always helpful
for me to use an old tool of assessment called the *Weed System.* The Weed
System utilizes four areas of evaluation which enable the assessor to logically look at the patient's problem. First is the *chief complaint,* or *subjective
information.* Then there are *objective findings* that support that complaint
(*objective information*). Then one uses the subjective and objective findings
to formulate an opinion or impression as to the patient's true problem. This
opinion or impression section is generally known as the assessment section

(*assessment information*). The final area of this system of evaluation is the formation of a plan of action to correct the patient's problem (*plan information*). It is my belief that this system of evaluation is invaluable when analyzing and developing a plan of treatment for any illness, be it physical, psychological, or spiritual. This tool is easy to remember because it utilizes the acronym *SOAP*:

S—subjective complaints
O—objective findings
A—assessment of subjective and objective findings
P—plan of action.

Let us consider suffering using this tool. Remember, the assessor must look at the person who is suffering from the physical, sociological, psychological and spiritual aspects to come to a valid conclusion about the patient's problem.

Subjective: the patient's chief complaint is that he is *suffering*. To properly understand what the patient means by *suffering*, we must consider the different types of suffering. Suffering may be called physical or mental, depending on whether it is linked primarily to a body process (physical) or a mind process (mental). Examples of physical suffering would be pain, nausea, or breathlessness. Examples of mental suffering would be anxiety, grief, hate, or boredom.

One must also consider the intensity of suffering and the patient's attitude toward suffering. Intensity of suffering comes in all degrees from mild to unspeakably insufferable. This is according to how the patient interprets his or her suffering. Examples are light or severe, avoidable or unavoidable, useful or useless, of little or great consequences, deserved or undeserved, chosen or unwanted, acceptable or unacceptable. It can be seen that to properly treat suffering you must carefully determine exactly what the suffering person is telling you about the nature of his or her suffering.

Objective: the signs of suffering. From the physical standpoint, such signs may include grimacing when an injured body part is moved, pain when touching an injured body part or weight loss due to some occult disease process. From the mental standpoint, there could be the presence of severe psychic stress manifested by anxiety or depression, mood swings as seen in bipolar patients, severe agitation, delusional thinking, and overt psychotic features including paranoia and hallucinations.

Assessment: matching the chief complaint with signs (physical or mental) that support the chief complaint. Then ask the question: is the suffering of the patient physical or mental or perhaps a combination of both? If signs point to a physical problem, then deal with it from a medical standpoint. If the signs point to a mental problem, be there for the patient. Touch them, pray for them, but do not rely on sympathy with the patient. Let God have His way in getting them through this period of mental suffering. Your job is to stay close to the patient, point them to Christ and the gospel, and be God's instrument of comfort to them.

Plan: As noted above, if the patient's suffering stems from a physical problem, deal with it medically. If suffering stems from a mental problem, then stay close to the patient with love and encouragement and let God comfort them through you. I read an article in one of my many medical magazines about a young lady who was a primary care physician. Her approach to the suffering patient was compassionate and to the point. The title of the article was: "I Hug, I Kiss, I Cry." Her care plan was to hug the patient if they needed that warm touch, kiss the patient if they needed it, and cry with the patient when they cried.

I see the need for this plan of care every day when I make rounds in the nursing homes God has given me the privilege to serve. Many mornings when I come through the front door, I find a line of smiling faces, some standing, some in wheelchairs, and some in their beds. I see their arms reaching out to touch me. What they are saying is hug me; kiss me; cry with me. It is my eternal prayer, however, that they are not reaching out to touch me but to touch the Jesus whom God has placed in me. Jesus is their greatest need! I am nothing, only a tool to spread His love and compassion to these sweet saints. Some do not even know my name or the name of their sons or daughters. But through you and me, I pray that they do see the one that trained us and prepared us to be there for them. Jesus!

End of Suffering: How does suffering end? It ends when you realize that your life is not your own. It is your Heavenly Father's life. It belongs to Him when you surrender to His love and compassion for you. He knows what suffering is all about. He suffered the most when His only Son hung on the cross to save us from sin and suffering. Can we do no less? If we can be about God's business of relieving suffering, then we can see that suffering turns into *joy*.

Conclusion

In summary, I would like to discuss several vital areas of concern for any caregiver of those that suffer. These areas are really vital to any child of God who seeks to help "others." This is the reason for our existence on earth—*ministry to others.* Two areas of primary importance must be understood if we are to aid those that are suffering.

Area 1: Proper Adoption of Four Christian Priorities

Four priorities must be placed in proper sequence for you to live life according to God's will and be prepared to minister to those that suffer.

Priority 1: **God**—Once a person comes to grips with the realization that God is the only infinite and eternal Being, having no beginning and no ending, the Creator and Sustainer of all things, the Supreme Personal Intelligence and Righteous Ruler of His universe; then and only then are you prepared to minister to those who suffer. We speak of *total commitment* to God's direction when we should be speaking of *total surrender* to God's will in our lives.

Priority 2: **Family**—God created the family and gave man responsibility for being the spiritual head of the household. Sadly enough, we are seeing the destruction of the family by Satan's powers. He attacks the family and attempts to take the family apart at the seams. Remember, this is priority number two—not three or four.

Priority 3: **Work**—God has molded you and sanded you and has given you gifts and talents that are to be used in ministering to others. He expects you to use these gifts and talents for *His work* at your job. He expects 100 percent utilization of those gifts and talents in the workplace.

Priority 4: **The Church**—Fellowship with other believers—is vital to the Christian life. God has not called us to walk with Him, raise our families and use our gifts in isolation. He has purposed that we share life, ministering to one another, joined together as "living stones" in a spiritual household of faith.

Area 2: Proper Adoption of Four Christian Principles

Principle 1: **Be in God's Word daily.** You cannot minister to a suffering patient without referring them to the *instruction manual* (the Bible). The Bible was given to man from God, revealing Jesus Christ, the Son of God, and God the Son, the only Savior (John 14:6). He is the center and the circumference. It is Christ—from Genesis to Revelation (John 5:39). Everything you need to know about ministering to the suffering patient is found in these pages. Everything that the one who suffers needs to know about how God can help him through the fires of suffering is in these pages. However, if you never open the pages of this precious gift from God, your education is incomplete and your ministry to those that suffer will be ineffective.

Principle 2: **Prayer.** This is probably the most underused tool that God has provided for those who suffer and those who minister to the suffering. Prayer is asking and receiving; it is talking with God. It is making your request known to Him in faith. Matthew 7:7 explains the simplicity of what prayer really is: "Ask and it shall be given you; seek and ye shall find; knock and it shall be opened unto you" (KJV). Our Lord instructs the believer to ask, seek and knock, because these three words cover the whole spectrum of prayer. Many times the answer to the relief of a person's suffering is only a simple prayer away. I remember again some very wise words that Adrian Rogers said about a powerful prayer that he used in his daily walk with God. The prayer was simply this. "Dear God, your will, nothing more, nothing less, nothing else." How simple and yet how powerful!

Principle 3: **Witness.** If you have truly been called to witness to those that suffer, your life must be a witness to the love and compassion that Christ shows to the suffering. There are essentially three requirements that I learned in medical school. Just remember the 3 "A's." First is *availability.* Be there beside the one that is suffering, love them, and pray for them. Second is *ability.* You must study the Scripture and learn God's ways so that they become second nature so to speak. Then you will have the ability to serve those that hurt and are suffering at any time. Third is *amiability.* Webster defines this as characteristics of a person who is kind-hearted and sweet-tempered. I have taken license and added the characteristic of compassionate.

Principle 4: **God's Will.** Continuously seek to be in God's perfect will as you minister to the suffering. Many may ask themselves: how do I know what God's will is for my life? Over the years I have listened to many sermons on seeking and knowing God's will. Some were complicated and some very simple. I like to take a simple approach when I try to understand something that will deeply affect my life and my ability to minister. For me, finding God's perfect will has two requirements. Requirement number one is this: Whatever I am thinking or doing for God must be *consistent with the Scriptures.* Requirement number two is this: The results of my actions must serve to *edify the body of Christ.* For me, if these two requirements are met in whatever I do, then I believe I am in God's will.

If you adopt these Christian priorities and principals for your life and you stay the course, God will bless your efforts to minister to those that suffer. My prayer is that I have shared things with you in this chapter that will be helpful to you as you minister to those around you that are suffering. God will honor your efforts and the legacy of kindness and compassion that you leave behind will not be lost.

CPSIA information can be obtained at www.ICGtesting.com
Printed in the USA
LVOW06s1213200315

431275LV00001B/4/P